Monograph 4

AMERICAN ETHNOLOGICAL SOCIETY

MONOGRAPHS OF THE
AMERICAN ETHNOLOGICAL SOCIETY

4

JOSEPH BRAM

AN ANALYSIS
OF INCA MILITARISM

UNIVERSITY OF WASHINGTON PRESS

SEATTLE AND LONDON

PRINTED IN U.S.A.

TABLE OF CONTENTS

Preface

This paper was submitted as a dissertation in partial fulfillment of the requirements for the degree of doctor of philosophy in the Faculty of Philosophy of Columbia University. It was successfully defended before this Faculty in May 1940. Thanks are due to the American Ethnological Society for having included this study in their series of monographs and for having partially contributed to the cost of publication.

The author wishes to express his profound gratitude to Professors Ralph Linton and William Duncan Strong for their guidance and encouragement in the preparation of this study. He is also obligated for helpful criticism to Dr. R. Bunzel, Professor G. Herzog, Dr. B. Mishkin, Dr. M. W. Smith, Professor F. Tannenbaum, Dr. G. Weltfish and Dr. K. A. Wittfogel.

No student of Andean society can pursue his research in this field without acknowledging his indebtedness to the valuable contributions of Philip Ainsworth Means as well as to the classical works of C. R. Markham and H. Cunow.

New York, May 1941

INTRODUCTION

The Method and the Problem

The treatment of historical evidence by scholars has been dominated by two basic attitudes. The one attitude puts emphasis on the unique and non-recurrent character of historical events; the second attempts to capture general trends and sequences with the object of formulating laws.

The first mentioned view restricts the field of history to the accumulation of reasonably well-established facts. Historians of this school have recorded the events and presented them in a simple descriptive or narrative manner with no other motive in mind than that of chronicling. Oakshott, the British historian, has expressed this attitude neatly thus: "The attempt to imagine and elucidate a past, lost and different world from that in which the historian lives, is, taken by itself, completely satisfying."

Closely associated with this approach is the belief that chance and individuality play a predominant role in historical sequences; in this connection a typical question raised is: "Who can dare to say that if Alexander or Mohammed had not existed some other Macedonian king or Arabian prophet would have upset the world?"

Ernst Troeltsch, who is one of the most extreme exponents of this latter point of view, has gone so far as to deny any possibility of a general philosophy of history that would be universally valid; he reasons that there is no justifiable concept of mankind per se, and, since each culture-group has its own set of values, it therefore has its own peculiar system of causal sequence.

This uncompromising insistence on the individual and non-recurrent nature of historical events is usually referred to as Historicism. Although this point of view has not always been acknowledged explicitly by all historical writers, it has, nevertheless, been their underlying philosophy in most cases.

The gradual broadening of geographical and historical horizons could not fail to focus the attention of historians on countless cases of structural and functional analogies between historical situations, sequences of events and social institutions. Awareness of these analogies and similarities compelled scholars to turn from a history conceived as a succession of events unique in time and space to the study of typical activities of men as social beings. This new and different orientation of historical thought reached its high point in development in the second part of the nineteenth century. A systematic survey of the many attempts to use historical and ethnographic data for the purpose of historico-sociological generalizations would not be pertinent here. It is sufficient to mention at this point the school of social evolutionism associated with Spencer, Lubbock, McLennan, Tylor, Lang, Lippert, and Morgan, and the conflict school of sociology identified with Gumplowicz, Ratzenhofer, and Oppenheimer.

This was a period of intensive and enthusiastic activity by theorists, in an era brimming with great hopes and expectations. Multifarious historical and ethnographic data were scrutinized to yield universally valid generalizations concerning the conditions of social growth, arrest, and disintegration. Although this period reached its maximum productiveness within comparatively recent times, it has now become clear that most of the theoretical achievements failed to stand the test of time. Unilinear evolutionary schemes collapsed, under the weight of contradictory evidence, soon after they were formulated; also, the conflict theories of the origin of the state were weakened by numerous qualifications limiting their universality.

The partial or total failures of sociological historians strengthened the advocates of pure historicism in their rigid convictions. Their profound knowledge of specific historical material enabled them to score easy triumphs at the expense of the theorists who used material from secondary sources. As a result of this struggle, pure historicism regained, at the beginning of this century, ground it had lost at the end of last century. This has been particularly true among American anthropologists (Boas, Kroeber, Lowie, Spinden, Wissler, and others).

This stimulating ideological conflict has contributed greatly to the clarification of theoretical and methodological issues. It has also brought nearer the appearance of a more circumspect historical philosophy combining the soundest elements of the two viewpoints. A familiarity with the trials and errors of this period has shown that there can be no facile road to sociological generalizations, and that every bit of theorizing has to be preceded by intensive studies of specific problems in the particular societies and epochs. On the other hand, it has become clear that significant theoretical results cannot be expected as an automatic outcome of numerous intensive, historical case studies. If valid historicosociological generalizations are to be attained at all, blind curiosity must give way to a directed analysis, and historical research must be organized about meaningful problems. Only then can a joint effort of historians serve the purpose of establishing a working typology of historical processes and of discovering functional relationships among them. Such an approach would allow historical science to make some progress beyond the defeatist positions of purely descriptive historicism. As to the selection of significant problems, students are naturally attracted to historical phenomena of universal occurrence. We can hope that in concentrating attention upon parallel studies of a few basic problems of universal importance they will eventually emerge with important synthetic statements.

One of the problems, which could be investigated in practically all the civilizations of the world, is the relationship between warfare and social and political institutions. We can assume that this relationship must have been of a reciprocal nature, in other words, one of a mutual interdependence. While wars are obviously deeply rooted in the social and political structure of societies, they in their turn exert an effect on and modify this very structure. In this study I have accepted interdependence between warfare and social and political institutions as a basic presupposition, and I have selected the pre-Conquest Andean world for a specific investigation of this relationship. An attempt is made here to view the state of the Incas in relation to the whole Andean area. The paucity of pre-Incaic and non-Incaic data necessarily limits the extent of historical depth that can be reached in the treatment of the problem. Nevertheless, it is important to see the state of the Incas as only one of the many political organisms of different levels of complexity, that flourished and died in this part of the world.

Any other civilization could have been chosen for the study of our problem, but the civilizations of the Old World offer special difficulties due to their very intricate genetic and cultural inter-connections. In the Old World, every interpretation of a series of historical phenomena of one society in terms of this one society must be preceded by a careful elimination of foreign elements, either intrusive or borrowed, that often distort the consistency of historical sequences. For example, since Iran and China, Mesopo-tamia and Ancient India, the Near East and North Africa, have all been exchanging cultural products and ideas for centuries, it would require a tremendous control of materials to precipitate out the phenomena of exchange and reciprocal influence.

Compared to other historians an Americanist finds himself in a privileged position. He deals with a continent which was settled by migrants from Asia from fifteen to twenty-five thousand years ago, and has remained isolated from the rest of the world until recently. These migrants reached America carrying the poor tech-nological equipment of neolithic man in the pre-agricultural stage. Thus, the settled agricultural existence that developed and spread over the American continent can be regarded as a purely local phenomenon. The high civilizations of the Andean area provide a particularly good instance of an isolated culture comparatively uninfluenced by outside historical developments. As Nordenskiold aptly phrased it, "The Peruvian civilization was built up of in-tensified Indian culture and not by anything additional or alien." Whatever influence Central America exerted on Peru, was dis-continued at a very early stage of Andean development. Lothrop, in discussing the museum collections in Lima, stated: "Almost every detected likeness to Central America in all parts of Peru occurred in types (of artifacts) to which Dr. Tello assigns an early date—as is also the case with the stratified remains from Ecuador."[1] The so-called archaic complex, consisting of agriculture, pottery, and weaving, may have come from Central America, but this had obviously taken place previous to the development of the Central American system of writing and the Central American calendrical systems.

This comparatively sheltered development of the high civiliza-tions of the Andes is particularly appealing to a sociologically

---

[1] Lothrop, Samuel Kirkland. *Pottery of Costa Rica and Nicaragua.* New York, 1926, vol. 2, p. 406.

minded historian. It offers a "laboratory" situation where a detached and isolated branch of humanity was given an opportunity to develop its own brand of social forms out of a limited number of simple elements.[2]

If social phenomena achieved under these circumstances of relative historical isolation, prove to offer structural and functional similarities to those observed in other civilizations, it would be difficult to explain away these similarities as mere coincidence. If the study of Incaic militarism undertaken here would show the presence of features of the type with which we are familiar in Old World history, such a discovery would be a contribution to our understanding of historical processes in general.

Sources of Inca History

History, by definition, deals with the past of human society. But it is not possible to salvage the past from the action of time and transmit it, in its totality, from one generation to another. It is not possible to know more regarding the past than available evidence allows us to believe. The sum total of historical evidence that reaches us represents after all but a fraction of the material and symbolic characteristics of the past, that survived the action of the blind forces of nature and the selective agencies of society.

In the case of archaeological remains, the selection of evidence is determined by the soil, the climate, and the resistance to the physical environment of various materials employed in the industries of man.

In the case of oral traditions, which include stories, legends, myths, and genealogies, the selection of evidence depends on a wide range of possible motives of a religious, a dynastic, an aesthetic, and various other natures.

Evidence recorded in writing is a result of an even more directly deliberate and purposeful action. Therefore, the interpretation of such evidence must make allowance for the author's personality, his objectives, and his vested interests.

Thus, whether our historical material has been preserved for us

---

[2] I am aware of the fact that some writers, such as Walter Krickeberg, Paul Rivet and J. Imbelloni, have insisted on seeing Asiatic or Oceanian influences in American high cultures. In the absence of concrete historical evidence supporting their claims, I feel justified in treating American high civilizations as a product of aboriginal development.

in the form of imperishable artifacts and structures, verbal traditions, or written records, we must realize that it is not more than a pale and somewhat distorted reflection of a past that can never be reconstructed in its entirety. If, in spite of this handicap, historians of dead civilizations have proved fairly successful in reconstructing dependable pictures of lost worlds, it may be due to the fact that there is more consistency and more logic in historical developments than we are willing to admit a priori.

The history of ancient Peru is based on a kind of material which more closely resembles an ethnographer's field-notes than written records of Old World history. The Spanish conquistadores who landed in Peru in the early sixteenth century were to a large extent in the position of contemporary anthropologists arriving in an unknown culture. They observed the outward aspects of this New World, made attempts to learn the language and to get explanations and historical evidence from "informants." However, the analogy ends here. While most field-workers in anthropology have little interest in distorting and falsifying the information they gather, the chroniclers of Peru were active participants in a movement of conquest and colonization and, as such, were motivated for selfish reasons and influenced by their group loyalties. They acted in their own interests as well as in the interests of the Church, the Army, or the political cliques to which they happened to belong. Thus, it is essential to become familiar with the life-story of the individual chronicler, in order to be able to estimate his impartiality and objectivity. A few of the chroniclers were men of native extraction, and their writings, in turn, were colored because of their solidarity with the conquered aborigines or some social sub-group among them. In both cases, purposeful distortion took place and vitiated the nature of the recorded evidence.

Vested interests and group loyalties were not the only causes of historical inaccuracies and distortions. The strong Occidental ethnocentrism was most powerful in preventing even the most scrupulous chroniclers from seeing aboriginal American conditions as they actually operated, and they could not help using images and concepts of their own Occidental culture. This last difficulty did not prove to be an insuperable obstacle, since, after all, this new Peruvian world was not so strikingly different in many major respects. Educated Spaniards of the sixteenth century found here a strong central government headed by a powerful monarch, a court teeming with dynastic rivalries, a well-organized bureaucracy and church hierarchy, and many other phenomena with which they were already familiar. As a matter of fact, they sized up this new world rather quickly, and a few years after landing, we find them busily engaged in local intrigues playing up individual ambitions and manipulating group interests.

In spite of their cultural preconceptions and handicaps, due to their various vested interests, the early chroniclers succeeded in handing down to us not only a very consistent picture of Inca society but even an account of Incaic history. This history is not a sequence of incredible and unexpected events that one might hesitate to accept at face value. On the contrary, behind different stories and accounts one can easily perceive institutions and processes known to the historians of the Old World.

The chroniclers of Old Peru do not always agree on specific facts and it is not easy to reconstruct an accurate historical sequence.[3] But, even if specific facts are often inaccurate as to details and the exact time and place of their occurrence, we can, nevertheless, distill out their institutional nature. The cumulative effect of identical accounts gives us confidence in the reality of the social institutions revealed by them and of the motivations involved in group actions.

Thus, when we read several accounts of tribal chiefs who gave their daughters in marriage to some other tribal chiefs in order to make peace and to establish friendly bonds between the tribes, we do not have to concern ourselves with the accuracy of the informants as to the names of the chiefs and of their daughters, and the dates of these events. What is vastly more meaningful is the significance which this practice lends to our understanding of the importance of the chieftainship on the one hand, and of the marriage bonds on the other hand.

This paper attempts to analyze the written records left by a score of the better known and more reliable Spanish chroniclers from the point of view of the problem as previously phrased. It must be pointed out that a vast treasure of material has not yet been made accessible to those working in this field. The monasteries

---

[3] See the Appendix, p. 80.

and archives of South America, as well as those of Spain and of the Vatican, are known to conceal countless documents of the epoch. The native languages of the Andean world have not as yet met with their Major Powell and Franz Boas. Furthermore, we may well anticipate that millions of half-acculturated Indians of the former Inca Empire are depositaries of valuable information, in the form of folklore, music, and social and religious "survivals." Thus, analytical work on the basis of the available material has rather a temporary value and must serve more as an incentive to future research than as a definitive interpretation of Inca history.

There is an abundance of biographical and critical literature devoted to each individual Spanish chronicler of ancient Peru. In this paper, I can only briefly characterize some of those whose writings I consulted in the preparation of my study.

Father Blas Valera is known to us indirectly, through Fernando Montesinos and Garcilaso de la Vega, who used his chronicles in their own writings. All Valera's original manuscripts had been considered lost; however, recently, *The Anonymous Chronicle by a Jesuit*, published by Jiménez de la Espada in 1879, was identified by experts as his work.[4]

Blas Valera was the son of a Spanish soldier of the Conquest who married an Inca lady of the court of Atahualpa. He was born at Chachapoyas in northern Peru about 1540, and lived in a number of places including Lima, Cuzco, La Paz, and Quito. When he was past fifty years of age, he left South America for Spain, where he died a few years later.

He had an opportunity to consult with a large number of the old Inca "keepers of the records", *quipucamayoc*, and the data obtained from them included the only known list of the ancient Peruvian kings who were the predecessors of the Inca dynasty. This list was preserved for us by Fernando Montesinos and is a most difficult document to interpret.

Garcilaso de la Vega used Blas Valera's material in the form of direct quotations. To judge by these quotations, Blas Valera must have been one of the best informed historians of the Inca civilization.

---

[4] Gonzalez de la Rosa, Manuel. El Padre Valera Primer Historiador Peruano. *Revista Histórica*, Lima, 1907, pp. 180-199.

GARCILASO DE LA VEGA was also a mestizo. His father was a Spanish army captain and his mother a woman of the Inca nobility. He was born in Cuzco in 1539; he remained in Peru until he was twenty, and in 1560 left for Spain where he lived to a ripe old age.

During his years in Peru, he became acquainted with a great many Inca stories and traditions. From Spain, he corresponded with his former school-mates, who provided him with historical material for his writings. Finally, as we stated above, he made use of the manuscripts of Blas Valera. He knew the Quechua language well and, in general, was well informed. He was remarkably accurate with regard to geographical names and topographical detail.

Garcilaso de la Vega was very proud of his Inca origins and identified himself with Inca nobility. In his "Comentarios Reales" he consistently white-washes the Inca rulers of all the accusations of tyranny and cruelty; he depicts them as the civilizers of the Andean world. His descriptions of the non-Inca coastal states refute this contention. His desire to idealize and glorify the Incas must be kept in mind when using his chronicles for historical reconstruction. The documentary value of Garcilaso de la Vega has been examined in detail by José de la Riva Agüero.[5]

Garcilaso de la Vega depicts the Inca territorial expansion as a gradual process and he distributes events of Inca history evenly among the different reigns of the ruling dynasty. The followers of this viewpoint are sometimes referred to as belonging to the Garcilasan School.

PEDRO DE CIEZA DE LEON was born in Sevilla in 1519 and came to the New World as a boy of fourteen. From that early age on, he led the life of a professional soldier and got an opportunity to see the western half of South America from the Valley of Cauca, in Colombia, to Lake Titicaca. During the seventeen years that he spent there, he kept records of everything he saw and heard; he took this self-assumed obligation very seriously, as can be seen from the following quotation:

Oftentimes, when the other soldiers were reposing I was tiring myself by writing. Neither fatigue nor the ruggedness of the country, nor the mountains and rivers, nor intolerable hunger and suffering, have ever been

---

[5] José de la Riva Agüero. *La Historia en el Perú.* Lima, 1910.

sufficient to obstruct my two duties, namely writing and following my flag and my captain without fault.[6]

Cieza de Leon was a keen observer and a man of considerable intelligence. His writings abound with analytical and interpretative remarks which are as valuable as the very rich factual material which they contain.

Several minor chroniclers deserve to be mentioned next to the above three great historians of Peru. These should receive recognition not so much on account of their greatness, but because they were among the first white men to see the Inca world.

One of them, FRANCISCO DE XERES, Pizarro's secretary, left a vivid account of the first episodes of the conquest. His description of Cajamarca and of Inca Atahualpa's camp is particularly interesting.

FERNANDO PIZARRO, the brother of Francisco Pizarro, wrote a Report to the Royal Audience of Santo Domingo which contains interesting data, including the description of Pachacamac, "the town of the mosque," and of the coastal valley provinces.

JUAN DE BETANZOS was also among the first conquerors and explorers of Peru. He arrived there with Francisco Pizarro and, after the initial campaigns, settled down in Cuzco. He married a sister of Inca Atahualpa and learned the Quechua language so well that he was appointed the official interpreter to several successive Viceroys. He left an unfinished history of the Incas, dated 1551, which was first published by Jiménez de la Espada in 1880.[7] It is a trustworthy historical document rich in descriptions, particularly in the case of the war of the Chancas.

PEDRO SARMIENTO DE GAMBOA was also a sixteenth century historian. He was an expert navigator, a man of science, a competent administrator, and an unscrupulous adventurer—all at the same time.

His writings are identified with the so-called Toledan School of Peruvian history. This school derives its name from Don Francisco de Toledo, who was viceroy of Peru from 1569 to 1581. Francisco de Toledo, who was one of the most ruthless enemies of the defeated Inca dynasty, engaged in a systematic distortion of Inca history.

---

[6] Pedro de Cieza de Leon. *The First Part of the Chronicle of Peru.* London, 1864, p. 3.

[7] Juan de Betánzos. *Suma y Narración de los Incas que los Indios llamaron Capacuna,* etc. Biblioteca Hispano-Ultramarina, Madrid, 1880.

He employed Sarmiento de Gamboa to write a history of the Incas, and in order to propitiate his master, Sarmiento de Gamboa depicted the Inca rulers as usurpers of power and tyrants of the people. In spite of his deliberate bias, his book is a very valuable chronicle. In his official capacity he had direct access to various sources of information and, in addition, read his manuscript to forty-two learned Incas for verification.

The Toledan School of Inca history is opposed to the Garcilasan School in that it assigns all the significant events of Inca history to the last few reigns. The object in presenting historical material in this manner was to show that the Inca rulers were monarchs of recent origin, and, therefore, were not entitled to the ancient rights to the throne of the Empire.

FATHER JOSÉ DE ACOSTA spent about fifteen years of his life in Peru (between 1570 and 1586). His *Natural and Moral History of the Indies* was published in Sevilla in 1590. It contains some valuable data on the economic life and religion of the natives of Peru. He recorded these on his extensive trips all over the country. Unfortunately, this book is also full of extremely naive stories and devotes much space to long irrelevant arguments.

POLO DE ONDEGARDO, who lived in Peru for more than thirty years (between 1544 and 1575), was a jurist and a statesman. He was appointed Corregidor of Charcas and later of Cuzco. He did extensive research work in the administrative methods of the Incas and was a great admirer of their political genius. He left several writings, the best known of which is his Report. This contains valuable data on land tenure, on the system of tribute collection, and on property.

Bishop BARTOLOMÉ DE LAS CASAS was a contemporary of the above XVIth century writers. He was born in Sevilla in 1474 and died in Cuba in 1566. He is regarded as a reliable historian of Peru in spite of the fact that he never lived there. Among his sources there possibly were some manuscripts which have since been lost. His compilation is relatively rich in data on pre-Inca society. It was published by Jiménez de la Espada under the title *De Las Antiguas Gentes del Perú*, in 1892. Bartolomé de las Casas was well known in his time as a great humanitarian and a champion of Indian rights.

CRISTÓBAL DE CASTRO and DIEGO DE ORTEGA MOREJÓN deserve special mention as authors of the only known description of the province of the Chincha Valley. Most of the chroniclers described the "sierra," but these two authors also gathered data on pre-Inca coastal society. In spite of their brevity they are very valuable. This chronicle was recently published by H. Trimborn with commentaries by W. Petersen.[8]

The greatest chroniclers of Peru wrote in the XVIth century, while Incaic traditions were still alive. The XVIIth century historians were more compilers than original observers and scholars.

Among them, JUAN DE SANTA CRUZ PACHACUTI YAMQUI SALCAMAYHUA occupies a particular place of interest because he was a full-blooded Indian. His *Relación de Antigüedades deste Reyno del Pirú*, dated 1620, was greatly estimated by Markham. However, this volume offers little information that is not available in earlier chronicles.

FATHER BERNABÉ COBO was also a seventeenth century writer. He spent more than fifty years of his life in Peru, and while there, traveled extensively. Although his *Historia del Nuevo Mundo*, published first between 1890 and 1895 in Sevilla, in four volumes, contains a wealth of data on the geography of the country and on the native agriculture and medicine, it is not rich in new historical material. As an historian, he belongs to the Garcilasan tradition and accordingly depicts the history of the Incas as a gradual process of growth.

FERNANDO MONTESINOS lived in Peru for at least fifteen years. He engaged in research on mining and while doing this work he explored all parts of the country. Later, he became Rector of the Jesuit Seminary in Trujillo. He was always interested in ancient Peru and purchased a number of historical manuscripts. His *Memorias Antiguas del Perú* contains the list of Inca rulers mentioned above, copied from the manuscript of Blas Valera. Although Montesino's writings are extremely unreliable, they nevertheless contain data on early Peru that are found nowhere else.

The purpose of this sketchy survey is to convey an idea of the background and personality of each of the principal chroniclers. It is, of course, far from exhaustive. The most comprehensive up-to-date bibliography and appraisal of Peruvian historical literature is to be found in Means' *Biblioteca Andina*.[9]

---

[8] Hermann Trimborn. *Quellen zur Kulturgeschichte des präkolumbischen Amerika*. Stuttgart, 1936.

[9] P. Means. *Biblioteca Andina*. New Haven, 1925.

I. TYPES OF SOCIAL AND POLITICAL ORGANIZATION IN THE ANDEAN AREA

The Andean Area before the Incas

A great many Spanish chroniclers would have us believe that the high level of civilization and the complexity of political organization found by the Conquistadores in Western South America had been created and developed by the Incas, out of a state of anarchy and complete savagery. They quote to this effect accounts which they heard from the natives of this part of the world.

Cieza de Leon's testimony is quite typical of this tradition:

> I often asked the inhabitants of these provinces what they knew of their condition before the Incas became the lords. On this they say that all men lived without order, and that many went naked like savages; that they had no houses, nor any habitations except the caves. . . .[1]

On this same point, Sarmiento de Gamboa commented:

> . . . although the land was peopled and full of inhabitants before the Incas, it had no regular government, nor did it have natural lords elected by common consent to govern and rule. . . . On the contrary all the people were scattered and disorganized, living in complete liberty, and each man being sole lord of his house and estate. . . .[2]

This state of affairs was characterized by incessant wars between neighboring groups, as Cieza de Leon tells us:

> . . . they made fortresses in the mountains called "pucara" out of which they came forth, using strange languages, to fight one with the other over the cultivable lands, or for other reasons. . . .[3]

---

[1] Pedro de Cieza de Leon. *The Second Part of the Chronicle of Peru*. London, 1883, p. 2.

[2] Pedro Sarmiento de Gamboa. *History of the Incas*, London, 1907, p. 37.

[3] Pedro de Cieza de Leon, *op. cit.*, The Second Part, p. 2.

According to Garcilaso de la Vega, these wars were extremely cruel "inasmuch as they ate each other as if they were brutes of different species."[4]

If we are to accept these and similar statements at their face value, we would have to believe the historical version of the Incas who regarded themselves as benefactors and civilizers of the benighted Andean Indians. This view of the Incas as "Kulturträger" is well illustrated by the following account by Cieza de Leon:

The Incas, reigning over them, considered their manner of living to be evil, and induced them, partly by menaces, and partly by favors to see the wisdom of ceasing to live like savages, but rather as reasonable beings, establishing themselves in towns. . . . In this way the Indians abandoned the pucaras in which they originally dwelt, and formed themselves into communities in towns, as well in the valleys of the coast as in the mountains. . . .[5]

Statements of this kind, which are usually found in the introductory chapters of the chronicles, must have satisfied the stylistic tendency of the chroniclers to give historical crescendo to their narratives, a simple archaic beginning developing gradually toward an impressive and magnificent conclusion.

These statements must also have been a direct reflection of the official version of Inca history which was created and circulated by the Incas themselves, for the rather obvious motives of prestige and self-glorification.

However, if we discount the emphasis that these accounts place on "savagery," "barbarism" and "cannibalism," and preserve the more sober factual statements, we obtain a picture of one of the simpler social types which the Incas had encountered in the process of their expansion. In the first place, all these "primitives" (i.e. from the point of view of the Incas) were agriculturists. All chronicles agree that they fought their wars for arable land. Besides, some chronicles also specify a struggle for sources of water, since their fields often depended on irrigation. When the first Inca Manco Capac descended into the Valley of Cuzco to take the land of the Alcabisas, his wife Mama Huaco advised him as follows:

---

[4] Garcilaso de la Vega. *The First Part of the Royal Commentaries of the Incas*. London, 1869–1871, Vol. 1, p. 60.

[5] Pedro de Cieza de Leon, *op. cit.*, The Second Part, p. 75.

. . . let us take all the water of the Alcabisas and then they will be obliged to give us the rest of their land. This was done and they took away the water. . . .[6]

Bartolomé de Las Casas also wrote of the struggle for land and for water:

In former times, before the Inca kings ruled over these lands, the inhabitants waged wars for land and for water. They had their settlements on high mountain tops where they had to carry their food with great difficulties. . . .[7]

A type of agriculture depending on irrigation, even on a small scale, implies a certain amount of group cooperation and of social cohesion. This can also be said of the fortification of the hill-tops and the erection of the *pucaras*, which must have been group undertakings.

It is difficult to visualize settlements of agriculturists who, surrounded by hostile neighbors and obliged to fight for their very existence, would not evolve some form of leadership, at least in time of emergency:

When it became known to the people of one district that some from other parts were coming to make war, they chose one who was a native, or he might be a stranger, who was known to be a valiant warrior. . . . Such a man was followed and his orders were obeyed during the war. When the war was over, he became a private man as he had been before, like the rest of the people, nor did they pay him tribute either before or afterwards, nor any manner of tax whatever. To such a man they gave and still give the name of Sinchi, which means valiant. . . .[8]

Fernando Montesinos describes how these temporary war leaders oftentimes became political "lords":

For purposes of defense the ayllus and families elected chiefs according as the occasions of war and peace offered themselves; with the passage of time some men by force and cunning gained advantages over the rest and began to lord it over them. . . .[9]

---

[6] Pedro Sarmiento de Gamboa, *op. cit.* p. 59.

[7] Bartolomé de las Casas. *De Las Antiguas Gentes del Perú.* Madrid, 1892, p. 41.

[8] Pedro Sarmiento de Gamboa, *op. cit.*, p. 38.

[9] Father Fernando Montesinos. *Memorias Antiguas Historiales del Perú.* Hakluyt Society, London, 1920, p. 3.

It is significantly revealing that the name of the second Inca ruler was Sinchi Rocca. Thus, his very name betrayed his position as war leader (sinchi).

There is a great temptation to trace all the origins of political authority in Andean societies to the concentration of power in the hands of war leaders. Much more evidence, however, would be required to make it a watertight proposition. The fact remains that all accounts of inter-group alliances in time of war were described by the chroniclers in terms of agreements concluded between chieftains.

Cieza de Leon relates of the alliance formed by the Colla tribes to resist Tupac Inca:

> The Collas, when they knew that Tupac Inca was marching against them in great power, sought help from their neighbours and assembled most of them with the determination to await his approach and to give him battle. . . . With the lords of their villages as captains, they advanced toward the position where Tupac Inca was encamped.[10]

The importance of the role of the chiefs in inter-group relations is revealed by one widespread Andean institution, namely, the marriage of one chief's daughter to another chief, as a token of peace and to consolidate friendly relations between two groups.

Fernando Montesinos, in describing the submission of the valley of Cuzco chiefs to the legendary Inca Manco Capac, tells us how in confirmation of peace and friendship, "they offered him in marriage the daughter of the most important of the lords."[11]

Fernando Montesinos wrote of another legendary Inca ruler, Huanacauri:

> . . . [he] still further strengthened his position by marrying a daughter of the lord of a village called Hillaca, in the Valley of Yucay. . . .[12]

A propos of Inca Capac Yupanqui's conquest, Sarmiento de Gamboa wrote:

> He forcibly subjugated the people of Cuyumarca and Ancasmarca, four leagues from Cuzco. A wealthy Sinchi of Ayamarca, from fear pre-

---

[10] Pedro de Cieza de Leon, *op. cit.*, The Second Part, p. 172.

[11] Fernando Montesinos, *op. cit.*, p. 9.

[12] Fernando Montesinos, *op. cit.*, p. 17.

sented his daughter, named Ccuri-hilpay to the Inca. . . . The Inca received her as his wife. . . .[13]

These instances demonstrate that the position of these "lords" and chiefs must have been of a sufficiently permanent character since the marriage of their children could serve as a guarantee of peaceful inter-tribal bonds.

The history of the Andean area is, in general, extremely rich in instances of inter-group alliances for defensive or offensive purposes. There is evidence to the effect that such alliances outlived sometimes the immediate military objectives, and continued on as political confederacies. Within these alliances, there existed an inequality in the relationships between different chieftains. One of the better known confederacies was that of the Chancas which was described by Garcilaso de la Vega:

> Under the general name of Chancas many other small tribes were included as Hancohuallu, Utunsulla, Uramarca, Vilca and others. The ancestors of these tribes came from a great distance, and overran many provinces until they reached that where they now live, which is the province of Antahuaylla. They conquered it by force of arms, drove the former inhabitants out, and forced the Quechua Indians into a corner, taking many districts from them. They also obliged these Quechuas to pay tribute, treated them tyrannically. . . .[14]

The magnitude to which a confederacy of this kind could grow can be seen from the fact that the Chancas once challenged the very power of the Incas themselves under the walls of Cuzco; it was there that they were finally defeated and lost their identity as a political unit.

It is known from various chronicles that the Chancas had a complex hierarchical system of chiefs of different degrees of importance and that at times there was an overlord over all of them.

The Collas of the region around Lake Titicaca also entered into more or less complex political formations. Cieza de Leon tells of a war between two Colla overlords, Zapana and Cari, and describes them as surrounded by their "friends," "vassals," and "principal chiefs."[15]

---

[13] Pedro Sarmiento de Gamboa, *op. cit.*, p. 69.

[14] Garcilaso de la Vega, *op. cit.*, Vol. I, p. 324.

[15] Pedro de Cieza de Leon, *op. cit.*, The Second Part, pp. 130–131.

When the Collas were defeated in a war with the Inca Yupanqui:

> ... having crossed the Desaguadero, all the principal chiefs assembled and took counsel together. They determined to send to the Inca and ask for peace . . . The most important among them were chosen to treat on this matter. . . .[16]

We lack more specific information on the structure and functioning of political confederacies of the Chanca and Colla type. Nevertheless, the information that we have about them shows them to be powerful political units, based on collaboration of tribal chieftains of unequal rank, and serving the purpose of defensive and offensive warfare.

The above fragmentary survey of political formations of the pre-Inca and non-Inca Andean world is based only on chronicles. We shall have to resort to archaeological evidence to get an idea of one of the highest types of political formations attained on the South American continent before the time of the Incas, the Early Chimu civilization which flourished in the valleys of the Santa, Viru, Moche, and Chicama Rivers, around 500 A.D.[17]

The Early Chimu were agriculturists living in densely populated valleys which were made fertile by an ingenious system of irrigation. They constructed miles of canals and ditches, erected huge truncated pyramids (probably for ritual purposes), built long defensive walls running inward from the sea in the high foothills of the Andes, and founded cities covering many square miles. They were expert weavers and potters, and used metals extensively for weapons and implements.

The realistic decorations on their pottery depict scenes of the life of the period. These give us some insight, however small, into their social organization. One of the decorative panels of an Early Chimu vase shows an important personage carried on litters by two litter-bearers. Many pots depict highly ritualized dances. Others show men wearing masks, and still others depict trumpeters and cupbearers. One painting reveals several women weaving, under the supervision of a man. Representations of warriors and

---

[16] Pedro de Cieza de Leon, *op. cit.*, The Second Part, p. 174.

[17] See P. A. Means, Ancient Civilizations of the Andes, New York, 1931, pp. 50–70; Thomas A. Joyce, *South American Archeology*, London, 1912; J. Eric Thompson, *Archeology of South America*, Chicago, 1936; Otto Holstein, "Chan Chan, Capital of the Great Chimu," *Geographical Review*, 1927, pp. 36–61.

of battle scenes are particularly abundant. Warriors are shown protected by different types of shields and helmets and armed with mace-like war clubs, slings, spears, spear throwers and very characteristic hatchets with broad blades. Some of the scenes depict them in hand-to-hand fighting with warriors of a different physical type, whose dress and armor are inferior to theirs.

With the exception of the Inca Empire, the above coastal civilizations represent the highest level of cultural and political development attained in South America. In this area the principle of political leadership developed apparently into a hereditary dynastic rule. The monarch was head of an intricate political structure. He must have been surrounded and supported by a large family, a priestly class, and by the army. The efficient maintenance of impressive public works must have required a high degree of social discipline, possible under the supervision of a bureaucracy. The specialization of technical, professional personnel must have detached large numbers of people from direct productive agricultural work, and created a highly stratified society. From the accumulated evidence, we can infer the existence of the following social and professional groups: the monarch and his immediate family, the priestly class, the army captains, numerous artisans of various kinds, and the commoners who were tillers of the soil.

In the early and late Chimu societies, we can be certain of the importance of the men who were at the head of the armed forces. The foundations of these coastal states were laid by military conquests. Regular and efficient collection of tribute from the conquered peoples was also secured through military control. Finally, the very existence of these states depended on the armies, which protected them from the war-like neighbours in the north (Tumbez, Cañar, and others), in the eastern Highlands, and in the south (the southernmost point being the impressive fortress of Parmunca).[18] Thus, although we are uninformed as to the intimate details of their social organization, such as forms of marriage, subdivision into clans, etc., we can gain to some extent an inferential idea of their political structure. We can also perceive with clarity the all-important part played by wars and warriors in the processes of their emergence, functioning, and growth.

This picture of the Early and Late Chimu civilizations is based

---

[18] Louis Langlois. "Parmonga." *Rev. Mus. Nac. Lima,* 1938, pp. 21–52, 281–307.

on the combined evidence offered by the realistic art and other archaeological material, as well as by the folklore. Other valleys of the Peruvian coast, as well as the highlands of Ecuador, Peru, and Bolivia were also important sites of advanced and complex societies. Unfortunately, however, the possibility of reconstructing the life of these societies is handicapped by the non-realistic character of their art and the scarcity and unreliability of their folklore.

The next important center of culture, south of the Chimu states, was located in the valleys of the Lurin and Rimac rivers. It was a thickly populated district with at least two important urban settlements, Pachacamac and Cajamarquilla. These cities reveal the existence of spacious plazas, courts, and halls. The residential section of Pachacamac was divided into four quarters. The region abounds with cemeteries where there still are thousands of un-excavated graves and with impressive ruins of temples and pyramids. Pachacamac was an ancient center of religion and played this role even at the time of its conquest by the Incas. We know little concerning the political structure of this area in ancient times. The Inca invaders found there a strong ruler, Cuismancu, whose power extended over numerous neighboring river valley states.

About three hundred miles south of Pachacamac there was situated another important center of ancient culture, which is identified with the valleys of Chincha, Pisco, Ica, and Nazca (Rio Grande). The Ica and Nazca river valleys are considered the site of the so-called Early Nazca culture. Some archaeologists regard it as more ancient than the Early Chimu culture, while others maintain a contrary point of view. The art of Early Nazca is predominantly ornamental and symbolic; consequently it is poor in the realistic elements that might give us some indications regarding the life of this period. The most remarkable feature of the Nazca area is the astonishingly intricate system of irrigation. There are found here indications of trade relations with the mountain folk, which can be inferred from the presence of obsidian, lapis-lazuli, and woolen textiles. Cotton was grown on the Nazca plains and gold was worked on a small scale. The sum total of archaeological evidence bespeaks a highly advanced and mature culture developed by a densely settled agricultural people who were dependent on irrigation.

The culture of Chincha valley was similar in many respects to Early Nazca. We have data on this center not only from archaeological sources but also from the chronicle by Cristóbal de Castro and Diego de Ortega Morejón, which refers to immediately pre-Inca times. According to this chronicle, the Chincha valley region was inhabited by a number of independent tribes which were divided into "ayllus" and presided over by strong chiefs. These tribes frequently engaged in warfare against one another.

When we leave the coast and survey the Andean highlands, we find evidence of advanced cultural developments extending from northern Argentina (the area of the Diaguites) up to the Kingdom of Quito mentioned above. While the archaeological relics of these highland cultures are rich and suggestive, the available historical and folkloristic material is thin and unreliable.

In the period between the sixth and tenth centuries there existed, according to Fernando Montesinos, a powerful and politically advanced civilization in the highlands. The two centers of this civilization were Tiahuanaco and Cuzco. Eventually it disintegrated and was followed by a period of troubles and catastrophes, from which emerged the state of the Incas. The ruins of Tiahuanco, Chavín, and several other localities in the highlands prove incontrovertibly that complex cultures preceded the Inca state; consequently Montesino's chronicles are not completely without basis in fact. However, they are so confusing as to make their use for historical reconstruction extremely difficult.

In this chapter, we have surveyed a whole range of social and political types and cultural centers found in the vast Andean area. Some of these are known to us from the Spanish chronicles, such as the Collas, Chancas, Incas, Late Chimu, and Chincha. Others are known from archaeological material only, namely, the cultures of Early Chimu, Pachacamac, Early Nazca, Tiahuanaco, and other highlands cultures.

The purpose of the above enumeration of several culture centers was to indicate the extreme antiquity and complexity of the Andean world, in which the Incas were the late-comers. Very significant developments must have taken place before the Incas appeared on the Andean stage, and archaeological evidence allows us to select several features that were common to most of them:

1. A system of agriculture largely dependent on irrigation.

2. A knowledge of weaving techniques employing llama wool (in the highlands) and cotton (on the coast).
3. A pottery with realistic and ornamental styles.
4. An ability to work in gold and in some cases in other metals.
5. An inclination toward massive structures of stone (in the highlands), and of adobe (on the coast).
6. A military defense employing permanent structures, namely, walls, pucaras, fortresses, etc.
7. An inter-regional economic exchange.

All these features taken together point to the existence of an advanced social and political development. However, vastly more research must be carried out in this area, before we will be in a position to breathe life into the relics of its past.

The "Ayllu" and the Dual Divisions

In the preceding pages we surveyed the range of social and political forms characteristic of the vast Andean area of the pre-Inca period. Chronologically, this survey covers the period of time between the consolidation of settled agricultural community life and the early reigns of the Inca dynasty. It may seem paradoxical that the earliest type of society on which we have data, namely, the Early Chimu, happens to be of a relatively complex structure, while some later types described by Spanish chroniclers were comparatively simple. Thus, it is not possible to treat the entire Andean area as one unit, and we are unable to outline the history of its social and political development. Instead, we can make an attempt to reconstruct a history of social and political development *typical for this area* and for its different societies, by piecing together items of information on various Andean groups at different stages of their existence. This would be a very dubious procedure were it not for the very striking homogeneity of the Andean world. The principal argument in favor of this approach is the universal distribution over this area of one basic social unit, a cell of Andean morphology, the ayllu.

The ayllu is found all the way ". . . from Cajamarca to Argentina in the South . . .," according to Max Uhle.[19] It is charac-

---

[19] "El Aillú Peruano." *Boletín de la Soc. Geogr. de Lima*, 1911, p. 81.

teristic of the Andean countries ". . . from Colombia to Chile
. . .," according to R. E. Latcham.[20] Philip Means says:

> All students of the subject recognize today that the ayllu . . . is the
> fundamental social group common to all Andean societies, great and
> small, ancient and modern. . . .[21]

The whole range of political forms found in this part of the
world looks not unlike a number of experiments with various com-
binations of ayllus. Even the Inca Empire can be regarded as a
large number of Andean Indian ayllus dominated by a few Inca
ayllus. However great the degree of complexity of the various
state-like forms of the Andean area may be, the fundamental unit,
the ayllu, is never obliterated; in fact, it has survived to the present day in the mountain villages of Peru and Bolivia.

What is an ayllu? Beuchat translates this term as clan, and the
German scholar Trimborn as Sippe, while the early Spanish lexi-
cographers translated it as "tribú," "genealogía," "casa," "fa-
milia," "casta," and "parcialidad de Indios." As we understand
it today, the ayllu should be regarded as a kin-grouping based on
real or imaginary bloodties, and at the same time as an economic
and social unit.

An ayllu usually traced its origins to a common mythical ancestor, who was a human being. The founder of an ayllu frequently
had an ally, who was his pact-brother. This pact-brother was
sometimes an animal, but more often a celestial body, a natural
phenomenon, or a geographical feature. However, in rites and
ceremonies he was represented frequently by a symbol which was a
living creature. Thus, the Sun of the Inca tribes was symbolized
by the legendary bird Inti. It was the duty of both the founder of
an ayllu and his ally to protect the ayllu and all its descendants.
Both were tutelary divinities, but only the founder was regarded
as the ancestor and progenitor, while his pact-brother was merely
a supernatural protector.

Latcham's testimony on this subject is of great interest:

---

[20] "The Totemism of the Ancient Andean Peoples." *Journal of the Royal Anthropological
Institute*, 1927, pp. 55–87.

[21] P. A. Means. *Ancient Civilization of the Andes.* New York, 1931, p. 286.

. . . neither the Incas, the Collas, nor the Araucanians thought they were descended from their totems. Each tribe had its founder or progenitor. The totem was the tutelary being with whom this founder had formed an alliance or pact, and both personages were well known and distinguished by all their members. . . .[22]

The ayllu took its name from the totem or from the symbol of the totem. The totem, or its animal representative, was believed to inhabit a particular object or a place, which became a point of worship, or a "huaca", as it was known in Quechua. The cult of the "huacas" was spread over the entire Andean area. The totem was inherited in the female line and membership in the ayllu was based on the matrilineal principle, according to Latcham. There is still, however, a doubt as to whether all Andean ayllus were organized matrilineally; there exist many indications of regional variation.

The great majority of the Indian ayllus were exogamous groups. There existed, however, cases of endogamous ayllus as well, due possibly to their geographical isolation which made it difficult to procure women from other ayllus. There also seem to have been ayllus which imposed no marriage restrictions on their members. In spite of these exceptions, exogamous, totemic ayllus (clans) can be regarded as the typical social form in the area under consideration.

The ayllu was also an economic and political unit. It was based on collective ownership and control of land, grazing fields, llama herds, forest rights, and sources of water. Christianity, and Spanish culture in general, eradicated the totemic features. The Incas forced local endogamy on the natives. But the combined influence of the Incas and of the Spanish did not destroy the economic basis of the ayllu. In a recent study, George M. McBride describes a few Bolivian peasant settlements, which preserve most of the economic features of the traditional Andean ayllu. The very location of the villages described by McBride is an indication of their relative antiquity:

It is in out-of-the-way corners of the country that community lands are still found: among the mountains where whites seldom penetrate, in

---

[22] Latcham, *op. cit.*, p. 69.

secluded angles of piedmont slopes, among the isolated peninsulas that border Lake Titicaca, on high inaccessible ridges, and out in semi-desert wastes on the open altiplano. . . .[23]

One of these ayllu communities, Calaque on Lake Titicaca, is composed of some three hundred families who own and cultivate their land in common. Although each member of the community has the legal right to sell his share in the common holdings, no one ever dares to do this since he would provoke the vindicative wrath of his neighbors.

In another collectivistic community, not far from La Paz, the Indians are so jealous of their rights that they permit no outsider to remain even overnight in their place. In this community, named Collana,

Each year there takes place the reallotment of the land; each day the cattle go out to pasture upon their common grazing land; each season, as in former times, the planting and the harvesting is carried on in voluntary co-operation. Bound up with their communal land-system is a complete social and political organization. They elect annually an alcalde from their own number and a cabildo (or council) to assist him. To these, their own officers, are referred all questions of public administration. They direct the distribution of the land. They regulate the use of the meager springs that supply the community with water.[24]

This picture corresponds to the idea we form of the ancient ayllu allotment system from the descriptions by Spanish chronicler:

They every year divided these lands of the community, in giving every one that which was needful for the nourishment of their persons and families. And as the family increased or diminished so did they increase or diminish his portion, for there were measures appointed for every person.[25]

Theoretically, an ayllu was also a territorial unit, that is, under climatic conditions sufficiently favorable to an agricultural economy based on maize, an ayllu occupied a natural ecological unit of territory and formed a unified settlement.

[23] George McCutchen McBride. *The Agrarian Indian Communities of Highland Boliva.* New York, 1921, p. 15.

[24] George McBride, *op. cit.*, p. 15.

[25] Father José de Acosta. *The Natural and Moral History of the Indies*, Vol. II, p. 420.

However, in the mountainous regions of the so-called "puna" where the economy was based on llama-breeding and on uncertain and insufficient crops of potato, oca and quinoa, the average ayllu, which consisted of approximately one hundred families, was forced to spread over a larger territory and eventually split into several small village communities.

On the other hand, the very fertile low valleys between the mountains and the river valleys of the coast made several ayllus gravitate around a common source of abundant economy. Sarmiento de Gamboa gives us a good example of such an arrangement:

> In this valley [of Cuzco] owing to its being fertile there were three tribes settled from most ancient times, the first called Sauaseras, the second Antasayas, the third Huallas. They settled near each other, although their lands for sowing were distinct, which is the property they valued most in those days and even now. . . .[26]

Thus, while a typical ayllu coincided with a village settlement, the real ecological situation was far more complex. Two halves of an ayllu that were forced to settle at quite a distance from each other, were likely to become estranged in spite of their common totemic bonds. On the other hand, several ayllus which were thrown together into a cooperative situation, such as that required by irrigation and other public works, or, which were forced to unite in times of danger for military defense, would gradually develop ties of solidarity and sometimes merge into a statelike alliance.

Whatever ecological or political unit we consider, we usually succeed in discerning in it one of the following:

1. A subdivision of an ayllu.
2. An entire ayllu.
3. A group of politically equal ayllus.
4. A powerful ayllu towering over a group of politically equal ayllus or, finally,
5. A more intricate aggregation of ayllus with different levels of subordination.

Whenever one of the larger political formations of the Andean area, such as a confederacy, a feudal state, or even an empire,

---

[26] Pedro Sarmiento de Gamboa, *op. cit.*, p. 40.

disintegrated and went down as a victim to historical fate, the many ayllus of which it was composed lost an ally, a protector, or an exploiter, or all of them at the same time. However, their inner existence which was based on agrarian collectivism and on group solidarity, was never profoundly affected by such a change. Since they were economically and socially self-sufficient and not dependent for their existence on ambitious political undertakings, the ayllus could easily revert to their isolated self-centered life. Of course, they always faced the eventuality of being forced into some new political combination, of submitting to a new master, and of being incorporated into a new statelike formation.

The rise and downfall of state-like formations were of more vital importance to those ayllus which assumed the leading role in the state-building process. If this process worked successfully, every member of the master-ayllu, rose in status and gained new political, economic, and military privileges and prerogatives. They became detached from direct productive agricultural work and developed gradually into a ruling aristocratic caste. The disintegration of the state, over which their ayllu presided, usually spelled their doom. Naturally, these nobles evolved systems of political and military control over their subjects, in order to prevent the loss of their superior position connected with the continued existence of the state.

We have presented the ayllu as a basic element in the Andean social morphology. The actual situation was somewhat complicated by the widespread principle of dual division, found in those settlements where several ayllus lived together. The two halves of the settlement, each one consisting of a few ayllus, were usually on "joking" terms; they engaged in sham-battles, and had different functions at ritual observances.

R. Latcham who studied a mass of material containing references to the dual divisions in the Andean area, admits that he has not been able to discover that the moieties were at any time exogamic; he states that, in general, "the original functions of the divisions had been forgotten at the time of Conquest."[27]

That this was the case can be seen from the following statement by Sarmiento de Gamboa:

---

[27] Latcham, op. cit., p. 57.

. . . before the Incas. . . in each tribe there were two divisions. One was called Hanansaya, which means the upper division, and the other Hurinsaya, which is the lower division, a custom which continues to this day. *These divisions do not mean anything more than a way to count each other, for their satisfaction. . . .*[28]

Although it is devoid of all functional significance the principle of dual division still survives in many Andean communities. McBride confirms this:

In the Department of Oruro . . . the parcialidad is the prevailing unit. It corresponds to the holdings of a community and has come to be recognized as a political as well as an agrarian unit. Each canton is divided into so many parcialidades, usually two or three, and each of these, in turn, contains a group of ayllus (from two to ten). *In many cases, as on other parts of the plateau, the ancient division of the people into aransaya and urinsaya (upper and lower town) is still retained.*[29]

The Inca ayllus settled in Cuzco, the capital of the Empire, were also divided into two moieties, the Hanan-Cuzco (upper Cuzco) and the Hurin-Cuzco (lower Cuzco). These moieties maintained privileged relationships with the Sapa-Inca (the Emperor) and the Coya (the Empress) respectively. They engaged in dynastic intrigues and quarrels as separate groups and formed separate units in war.[30]

Means has advanced a theory concerning the origins of the dual divisions in the Andean area. According to him they

. . . arose out of conquests made by an expanding ayllu in territory already occupied. In such a case the victors would constitute themselves into the "Hanan" moiety of the valley invaded and would leave the native folk in a group apart called "Hurin." This, almost beyond question, was the original form and reason of the moieties.[31]

I find it difficult to subscribe to Means' conquest-theory of the origin of the moieties in the Andes. His explanation does not take into account the fact that dual divisions were an extremely wide-

---

[28] Pedro Sarmiento de Gamboa, *op. cit.*, pp. 37–38.

[29] George McBride, *op. cit.*, p. 18.

[30] Thus, in the civil war between the two sons of Inca Huayna Capac, Huascar was supported by the Hurinsuyus and Atahualpa by the Hanan-suyus.

[31] P. Means. *A Study of Ancient Andean Institutions.* 1925, p. 439.

spread institution in South America where they were found among the Gês tribes (Ramkokamekran, Cherentes-Akuä, and Kaingang), the Bororó of the Rio Vermelho and Rio das Garcas, the Tupian tribes (Mundruku, Parentintin, Tembe), the Arawakan tribes (Palikur, Tukuna), and, as for the Andean peoples, among the Quechua, Aymara, Canari, Uro-Chipaya, and Chibcha. These dual divisions are most probably common in origin although their genetic relationship may go quite far back to archaic times.[32]

The complex of phenomena associated with the dual divisions in South America is of a ritual, ceremonial, and symbolical nature, and there are few significant economic or social functions attached to them. As for the Cuzco moieties, their transformation into political factions seems to be a very late development, that can be traced to no past conquest of one over the other. Means does not present any evidence in support of his theory, which is apparently based on pure conjectural reasoning.

We must hope that a methodical survey of all structural and functional similarities among the wide-spread dual divisions in South America, will eventually be elucidated through a new historical theory of their common origins.

As far as our analysis of the social and political forms of the Andean peoples is concerned, we can affirm that the division of larger settlements into moieties did not play any significant role in their political or economic history.

---

[32] Josef Haeckel. "Zweiklassensystem, Männerhaus und Totemismus in Südamerika." *Zeitschrift für Ethnologie*, 1938, pp. 426–454.

II. Territorial Expansion of the Inca State

The Beginnings of the Inca State

There exist various theories concerning the origins of the Incas, based on the chronicles as well as on linguistic evidence. Several accounts mention the fact that at the court they spoke a language which was unknown to the commoners and forbidden to them, and which was consequently not the Quechua. The exact provenience of the Incas is not relevant to our main problem. It is of interest, however, to note that the Incas were outsiders to the valley of Cuzco which they penetrated as invaders. In order to do that they had to force some of the settlers of this exceptionally fertile valley into submission and compel others to emigrate elsewhere. Testimony to this effect is contained in the official minutes of the investigation carried out in 1572, on the orders of the Viceroy Don Francisco de Toledo, by several officials and an interpreter. The investigators questioned five Indians of the ayllu Sausiray, five of the ayllu Antasayac and four of the ayllu Alcaviza. Five of these informants were men over seventy-five years of age who had spent their early years under the reign of the Inca Huayna Capac, predecessor of the last Inca. The ayllus to which these Indians belonged were settled at the time of the investigation in the neighborhood of Cuzco. The informants were asked how much they knew of the times preceding the invasion of the Inca ayllus in the valley of Cuzco.

. . . all joined in answering the third question and told that they had heard it said by their ancestors and parents that the first Inca, who called himself Manco Capac had cunningly forced his way into the residence of the above-mentioned three ayllus and had flattered his way into their confidence with smooth words. Then during the night he penetrated with his people by force into their lands. When the Indians of the three ayllus showed resistance toward him, Manco Capac and his people treacherously murdered many of them. It is because of the arable land in which Manco Capac and his people established themselves that the strife occurred. Every day his ranks swelled and his followers kidnapped the Indians of the ayllu of the Alcavizas in order to kill them because they opposed his claims to their property. At no time did the three ayllus recognize and respect him as their master. His successors treated them in the same way after his death. . . .[1]

This very vivid account describes how three ayllus that lived on the lands of the valley of Cuzco capitulated gradually under the pressure of the Inca invasion. In this case, land for agriculture seems to have been the objective of the Inca ayllus, although there may have been the question of tribute as well, which were to be paid by the conquered to the invaders.

From later history, we learn that the valley of Cuzco and the immediate country around it became the very heart of the Inca Empire. Under these circumstances, it is remarkable that although the three ayllus mentioned above were assimilated by the Incas and incorporated into their state, they nevertheless preserved their ayllu identity through four centuries of domination by the Incas. This instance corroborates the statement made in the preceding chapter to the effect that the ayllus which entered into the composition of the Empire of the Incas, and of similar Andean states, were autonomous and indestructible cells of the Andean social morphology.

It also means that Inca wars were not campaigns of annihilation but wars of conquest. The natives were forced to give up part of their arable lands and to submit to the authority of the Incas. In the later stage of Inca history, the process of incorporating the conquered provinces into the Empire developed into a very elaborate system of administrative, economic, and military measures.

From its very beginning, the history of the Incas has been a long narrative of successive wars and conquests. As Cieza de Leon puts it:

. . . In Peru they talk of nothing else but how some came from one part, and some from another, and made themselves masters of the land of their neighbors by wars and battles. . . . The Incas, it is well known, made themselves masters of this kingdom by force and intrigue. . . .[2]

---

[1] "Informaciones acerca del Señorío y Gobierno de los Incas hechas por mandado de Don Francisco de Toledo, Virey del Perú." Vol. 16 de la *Colección de Libros Españoles Raros y Curiosos*, p. 232.

[2] Pedro de Cieza de Leon, *op. cit.*, The First Part, p. 409.

However, the conquests of Indian ayllus were never definitive and required permanent vigilance on the part of the Incas.

. . . [the Incas originally] did not place garrisons in the places they subdued, so that when the Inca, who had conquered these people died, they rose in arms and regained their liberty. . . . the subjection only lasted while the lance was over the vanquished, and that the moment they had a chance they took up arms for their liberty.[3]

At this early period of their history, the Incas were already obliged to take measures to prevent the conquered provinces from regaining their independence. This continued to be one of the principal preoccupations throughout their history and brought into existence an elaborate system of communications, police, and military garrisons.

We have evidence to the effect that during the early reigns of the Incas they often had to conclude alliances for offensive wars, for example, Polo de Ondegardo spoke to some native of whom he writes:

. . . [they] retained the recollection of the time when the Canas and Canches . . . were paid to go with the Incas to the wars, and not as vassals following their lords. . . .[4]

In the later periods of their history, their problem was not so much to look for "foreign" alliances, although there were many such cases, as to solve the problem of securing the loyalty of the conquered ayllus and their chiefs in time of war. Since they were badly in need of the military cooperation of these chiefs (curacas), they maintained them in the roles of "indirect rulers" and encouraged them to carry on through a system of economic rewards and honors.

Thus, we have seen that the problems of (a) the incorporation of the conquered peoples into their state, (b) the prevention and suppression of revolts, and (c) the conclusion and consolidation of foreign and inner alliances for military purposes, must have made their appearance at the very first steps in the formation of the Inca state. The solutions and techniques of political domina-

---

[3] Pedro Sarmiento de Gamboa, op. cit., pp. 82–83.

[4] Polo de Ondegardo. Of the Lineage of the Yncas and How They extended their Conquests. London, 1873, p. 152.

tion must have emerged gradually through a trial and error method, until they finally reached the degree of elaboration and of efficiency known to us from the descriptions of the last Inca reigns.

The Policies of Incorporating Conquered Lands

Let us consider a non-Inca province soon after it had been over-run by the victorious Inca warriors. That will allow us to see the Inca imperial system in action and to ascertain in what way pre-Inca social and political forms were affected by the accession of a new province to the Empire. It should be pointed out that the Incas considered the land of their enemies as future domains and their enemies as future subjects. This attitude toward their ene-mies accounts for an unusually small amount of depredations caused by the Inca armies in the occupied lands.

In many [provinces] which were conquered by force of arms the order was that little harm should be done to the property and houses of the vanquished; for the lord said, "They will soon be our people, as much as the others." For this reason the war was made with as little injury as possible, although great battles were often fought, where the inhabitants desired to retain their ancient liberty and their religion and customs, and not to adopt new ways. . . .[5]

Whenever possible, the Incas preferred to occupy a province peacefully. Before dispatching an army against an enemy, they often resorted to negotiations and an appeal to reason. Promises of fair treatment to the conquered, were mixed with undisguised menaces and the success of diplomatic negotiation was often due to the presence of huge concentrations of Inca troops close to the border of the coveted land. Cieza de Leon's accounts give a good idea of such policies:

When the road that should be taken and the necessary measures were decided upon, the Inca sent special messengers to the enemy to say that he desired to have them as allies and relations, so that with joyful hearts and willing minds they ought to come forth to receive him in their prov-ince, and give him obedience as in the other provinces; and that they might do this of their own accord he sent presents to the native chiefs. By this wise policy he entered into the possession of many lands without war. . . .[6]

---

[5] Pedro de Cieza de Leon, *op. cit.*, The Second Part, p. 49.

[6] Pedro de Cieza de Leon, *op. cit.*, The Second Part, p. 48.

The combination of intimidation by force and of friendly persuasion is illustrated strikingly by the following citation from Garcilaso de la Vega:

> While the Inca was in the Collas, he ordered 10,000 men of war to assemble there in the ensuing summer. When the time came he appointed four masters of the camp, nominated a brother of his own . . . as general of army, and ordered him, in concert with the other captains to proceed with the conquest. All five were strictly enjoined on no account to fight the Indians, but, in accordance with the tradition of his father *to induce them to submit by kindness and persuasion.*[7]

The "appeal to reason" was usually addressed to the native chiefs. Cieza de Leon describes a case of negotiations of that kind:

> The Great Tupac Inca had long heard of the fertility of the coast valleys and of their beauty. . . . He now determined to send messengers with presents for the principal men, and a request that they would receive him as a friend and comrade. . . . He said that when he passed through their valleys, he would not make war if they desired peace, that he would give them some of his women and cloths, and would take theirs in exchange, with other things of a like nature . . . and that he was not cruel nor bloodthirsty, nor did harm to any except those who were troublesome and opposed themselves to him. . . .[8]

The cooperation of the native chiefs was of such importance to the Incas that they were ready to forgive a chief of a conquered province even after he had opposed them and was defeated. When, after a very long and cruel war, the Great Chimu submitted to the son of the Inca Pachacutes, who headed the Inca army, the prince said to the Great Chimu:

> . . . that all the past was forgiven, that he had not come to that land to deprive its chief of estate and lordship. . . . In proof of what he said, and lest the Chimu should fear that he had lost his estate, the Inca freely granted it to him, to hold in perfect security. . . .[9]

Not only were the local chiefs allowed to keep their estates, but they themselves were incorporated into the Inca administrative system, and, together with their families, formed a hereditary

---

[7] Garcilaso de la Vega, *op. cit.*, Vol. 1, pp. 171–172.

[8] Pedro de Cieza de Leon, *op. cit.*, The Second Part, p. 183.

[9] Garcilaso de la Vega, *op. cit.*, Vol. 2, p. 200.

local nobility with bureaucratic and military functions. This was a real system of "indirect rule" not unlike that of British India or French North Africa of our time.

The local chiefs of the conquered provinces, known as curacas in Quechua, played the role of intermediaries between the central government and the subjects of the vast Empire. The loyalty of their peoples was thus insured by the curacas to the state of the Incas, while their own loyalty was guaranteed by a system of rewards and punishments.

Their sons were brought to Cuzco where they remained at the court of the Inca. They learned the language of their new masters and were trained in administrative techniques and in the rituals of the state religion. As long as they stayed in Cuzco, they were tacitly considered hostages for their fathers' loyalty to the Empire.

The daughters of the curacas were admitted to the provincial "Houses of the Chosen Women," *Acllahuasi*, which was considered a great honor. Upon graduation from these institutions they either married nobles or took permanent places in the hierarchy of the Cult of the Sun.

The curacas themselves were consulted by the Incas on various administrative affairs. Carcilaso de la Vega tells us that:

... the Incas ordered that in all things, which were not contrary to their own laws and ordinances, the wishes of the Curacas of the different provinces should be considered.[10]

The curacas were not given a chance to indulge in a retired existence on their lands. As Garcilaso de la Vega tells us, they had to keep in close touch with the court:

... the Curacas lords and vassals, visited the Inca on the principal festivals of the year ... and on the occasion of triumphant celebration of victories, and when the heir to the throne was shorn and named, and on many other occasions during the year. ... .[11]

The brothers and other male relatives of the curacas were appointed priests of the Cult of the Sun, which was invariably introduced into the conquered provinces.

---

[10] Garcilaso de la Vega, *op. cit.*, Vol. 1, pp. 246–247.
[11] Garcilaso de la Vega, *op. cit.*, Vol. 2, p. 22.

The curacas and their families were exempt from all tributes but whenever they visited Cuzco, they were expected to present the Inca

. . . with all the gold and silver and precious stones that their Indians could collect when they had no other work to do. . . .[12]

The native troops of the Inca Empire were usually organized by provinces and were headed by their corresponding curacas, who in turn received orders from the Inca generals. Thus, in war as well as in peace, the hold of the curacas on their subjects was utilized by the state.

It must be made clear that the term curaca covered all the ranks of native nobility, from the war leaders, sinchis, of a small and weak ayllu, to the head of the powerful Chimu state. The Incas were a hierarchy-minded people, and whenever they incorporated a local chieftain or a ruler into their imperial administrative organization, they gave him a position in their hierarchy which corresponded approximately to his previous native rank and place.

In the administrative subdivision of the Empire, based on their well-known decimal system, the curacas were given command over groups of 100, 500, 1000, and 5000 men, in keeping with their former power. Subdivisions of more than 5000 men were headed by officials of Inca blood.

It has always been a moot question how this decimal system of administrative organization could cut across the more natural tribal, regional, or economic units of the Empire. It is not at all improbable that the above decimal classification was not meant to be understood literally but only as a conveniently approximate scheme.

We have applied the term "indirect rule" to the methods that the curacas used to influence the natives in the interests of the Empire. The *direct* methods of consolidating the Inca grip over the conquered lands and peoples were still more numerous and effective.

Among these, roads should be mentioned as one of the most important conditions of control over an annexed territory. The roads built by the Incas were used mainly for military purposes. The economic interdependence of the various provinces of the

---

[12] Garcilaso de la Vega, *op. cit.*, Vol. 2, p. 22.

Empire did not require such an elaborate network. The main road from south to north was not warranted by any economic necessity. The exchange of products occurred mainly between the mountains of the east and the coastal zones of the west.

As is well known, there was no money in the Andean economies, and commerce was quite insignificant. Whatever barter did take place, was limited to regional markets, so that roads of great length were superfluous for the existing commerce.

The function of the roads becomes more apparent if we point out that all private travelling was strictly prohibited under the Incas. As Bartolomé de las Casas tells us:

> It has been ordered that no Indian should go from one part of a province to another without the knowledge, permission or order of his lords, governors or superiors; and those who disobeyed, and traveled without permission were punished very strictly. . . .[13]

Thus, the roads, which were unimportant for commerce and unused by the commoners, served one main function; they placed the central government within striking distance of peripheral provinces that had been conquered. At the same time, they made possible concentration of troops in the border regions for purposes of further military expeditions.

Although we have a great deal of information on the system of roads which the Spaniards found in Peru, it has thus far been impossible to ascribe their construction to any definite periods in Inca history. It is not improbable that some of these roads were build previous to the Incas. However, the fact remains that they were great road-builders, which helped them a great deal to control their far-flung possessions.[14]

Communications between the provinces and the capital were maintained by a system of post-runners, chasqui, and by a less well-known method of signalling with watchfires on hill-tops. Roadhouses, provided with stores of food, and bridges, wherever necessary, should also be mentioned in connection with the problem of communications.

The political and military control of the country was facilitated

---

[13] Bartolomé de las Casas, *op. cit.*, p. 184.
[14] Alberto Regal. *Los Caminos del Inca en el Antiguo Perú*. Lima, 1936.

by the Incas' familiarity with the art of cartography. Garcilaso de la Vega tells us that:

. . . with respect to geography they understand very well how to paint and make models of each kingdom, and I have seen these models, with the towns and provinces depicted on them. I saw a model of Cuzco, with part of its province, and the four principal roads, made of clay and small stones and sticks. The model was according to scale, and showed the large and small squares, the streets whether broad or narrow, the wards down to the most obscure houses, and the three streams which flow through the city. It was indeed a piece of work well worthy of admiration; as well as the model of the surrounding country, with its hills and valleys, ravines and plateaus, rivers and streams with their windings, so well delineated that the best cosmographer in the world could not have done it better . . .[15]

The fact that these models were not toys, but were actually used for administrative purposes, is shown clearly by the striking account in the chronicles of Sarmiento de Gamboa:

[Pachacutec Inca Yupanqui] ordered visitors [visitadores in Spanish meaning inspectors] to go through all the subdued provinces with orders to measure and survey them and to bring him models of the natural features in clay. This was done. The models and reports were brought before the Inca. He examined them and considered the mountainous fastnesses and the plains. He ordered the visitors to look well to what he would do. He then began to demolish the fastnesses and to have their inhabitants moved to plain country, and those of the plains were moved to mountainous regions so far from each other, and each so far from his native country, that they could not return to it. Next the Inca ordered the visitors to go and to do with the people what they had seen him do with the models. They went and did so. . . .[16]

This example brings us to the consideration of one of the most important imperial policies of the Incas—the resettlement of the conquered populations. The resettlement and the selection of people for transportation from one province to another were dictated by various reasons in different cases. In the instance mentioned anove, inhabitants of the mountains were resettled in the plains where the topographic conditions were such as to expose

---

[15] Garcilaso de la Vega, *op. cit.*, Vol. 1, p. 190.
[16] Pedro Sarmiento de Gamboa, *op. cit.*, p. 120.

them to control by the Incas and make uprisings against them more difficult. The abandoned mountain settlements were handed over to loyal and dependable subjects of the Empire, while the resettled natives were removed far away from their traditional neighbors; this obviously prevented any possibility of a concerted action against the conquerors.

The resettled natives were usually removed to a loyal district. Sometimes, however, it was found more practical to reverse this process, transplanting faithful Inca subjects to newly conquered regions. In such cases the "mitimae" (plural of mitimac) were given the right of policing the natives among whom they were settled by the government.

> The Inca gave the colonists authority and power to enter the houses of the natives at all hours, night and day, to see what they said, did or arranged, with orders to report all to the nearest governor, so that it might be known if anything were plotted against the government of the Inca. . . .[17]

Cieza de Leon's account gives the same idea of the functions of these mitimae:

> Among the colonists there were spies, who took note of the conversations and schemes of the natives, and supplied the information to the governors, who sent it to Cuzco without delay, to be submitted to the Inca. In this way all was made secure, for the natives feared the mitimae, while the mitimae suspected the natives, and all learned to serve and to obey quietly. . . .[18]

In exceptional cases the mitimae themselves were kept in check by the natives in the interest of the central government. Cieza de Leon tells us that:

> . . . if there was any disturbance among the mitimae themselves they were attacked by the natives. . . .[19]

Apparently the Indians did not relish the idea of being resettled to new lands.

---

[17] Pedro Sarmiento de Gamboa, *op. cit.*, p. 121.
[18] Pedro de Cieza de Leon, *op. cit.*, The Second Part, p. 68.
[19] Pedro de Cieza de Leon, *op. cit.*, The First Part, p. 150.

. . . in order that they [the mitimae] might take such banishment with good will, [the Incas] . . . did honor to those who were selected as emigrants, gave bracelets of gold and silver to many of them, and clothes of cloth and feathers to the women. . . .[20]

We have now discussed the resettlement of subjugated natives and of faithful subjects of the Empire for the purposes of maintaining peace and establishing security. However, emigrants were sent to colonize new lands for purely economic motives as well.

Garcilaso de la Vega gives us the following description of the Inca colonization policies:

In the course of their conquests the Incas found some provinces to be naturally fertile, but thinly populated. To these districts they sent Indians who were natives of other provinces with a similar climate. . . . On other occasions, when the inhabitants of a locality multiplied rapidly, so that their province was not large enough to hold them, they removed a certain proportion of the people to some other distict.   They also removed Indians from barren and sterile tracts to such as were fertile and prolific, with a view to the benefit of both of those that remained and of those that went. . . .[21]

To what extent climatic considerations were taken into account in the transfer of populations stand out clearly from another citation from Garcilaso de la Vega:

The Inca took the Indians of Nanasca and transported them to the banks of the river Apurimac, near the high road from Cuzco to Rimac (Lima). For that river flows through a region which is so hot that the Indians of the cold and temperate climate of the Sierra soon sicken and die in it. . . . It was therefore forbidden to send Indians of the Sierra to the Llanos because they would certainly die in a few days. The Inca, mindful of this danger, took Indians from one hot climate to inhabit another. . . .[22]

In addition to the colonists transplanted by the Incas for political or economic reasons, a special category of mitimae made up garrisons under Inca captains. Their main role was the defense of the frontiers of the Empire. They were located on the eastern slopes of the Andes, bordering on the lands of the Chunchos, Moxos, and

---

[20] Pedro de Cieza de Leon, *op. cit.*, The Second Part, p. 68.
[21] Garcilaso de la Vega, *op. cit.*, Vol. 2, p. 213.
[22] Garcilaso de la Vega, *op. cit.*, Vol. 1, pp. 268–269.

Chiriguanos, northward of Quito adjacent to the province of Popayan, in Chile, and in many other places. Cieza de Leon gives us a good idea of how these garrisons were recruited and provided with provisions. He writes:

In order that the burden of war might not fall upon one tribe and that they might not be able quickly to concert a rising or rebellion, it was arranged that the mitimae should be taken from provinces that were conveniently situated, to serve as soldiers in these garrisons; whose duty it was to hold and defend the forts, called "pucaras," if it should be necessary. Provisions were supplied to the soldiers of the maize and other food which the neighboring districts paid as tribute.

The recompense for their service consisted of orders that were given on certain occasions, to bestow upon them woolen clothing, feathers, or bracelets of gold and silver, after they have shown themselves to be valiant. They were also presented with women from among the great number that were kept in each province, for the service of the Inca, and as most of these were beautiful, they were highly valued. Besides this the soldiers were given other things of little value, which the governors of provinces were required to provide, for they had authority over the captains whom these mitimae were obliged to obey. . . .[23]

The Changes in the Social Life of Conquered Peoples

Until now we have omitted consideration of the transformations, resulting from Inca administration, inside the village communities. Previous to the conquest and incorporation of an ayllu or a group of ayllus into the Empire, the Indians lived in a small and circumscribed political, social, economic, linguistic, and religious world.

(*a*) Politically, the native owed allegiance to a sinchi or a curaca whom, in most cases, he knew personally and who was not a stranger to his group. When his settlement was in danger and he had to defend it, the nature of such a war was obvious to him. He fought in a familiar environment and for his own cause.

(*b*) Social relationships within an ayllu were those of an almost unstratified community with collective landownership. The curaca and his family formed the only nobility, while the mass of commoners were all equals. The possibilities of economic and social

---

[23] Pedro de Cieza de Leon, *op. cit.*, The Second Part, pp. 69–70.

advancement were practically non-existent, and this must have insured a considerable degree of stability in inter-personal relations.

(*c*) Economically, a village community was a self-supporting unit, which engaged in a moderate amount of barter with neighbours. The curaca was exempt from labor in the fields, but it must have been relatively simple for a middle-sized community to support him and his family.

(*d*) The multiplicity of linguistic stocks in the Andean area limited the natives to associations with related groups or tribes.

(*e*) This was even more the case in their religion. Most ayllus limited their cult to their own tutelary and totemic supernatural beings, and only occasionally displayed some interest in the cult of the neighbouring ayllus.

These five observations concerning the Andean ayllu-communities are literally true only of those that lived isolated and were not members of any alliances, confederacies, or feudal states. Such a state of isolation and of complete independence was not prevalent in this area. It is useful, however, for the purposes of analysis to understand first the above *simplified typical case*. Numerous changes occurred under Inca rule.

(*a*) When a native community was incorporated into the Inca Empire, the Indian passed from membership in a more or less democratic village community to complete subjection to a distant and a terrible alien master. Occasionally, a representative of this ruler visited the settlement in order to converse, in a strange language, with the curaca and issue orders.

While inter-group wars between the ayllus ceased with the arrival of the Incas, men from the villages were drafted now for wars in distant lands and for unknown causes. This was a kind of war that differed from the familiar and traditional fighting that took place among neighbors for lands and water sources.

(*b*) With the Inca invasions arose new social groups. Selected girls were taken away from their families and brought up in the "Houses of the Chosen Women". There they lived in seclusion and formed a group by themselves. Eventually, they married into the nobility or became priestesses of the Cult of the Sun.

A certain number of men were drafted as servants; they formed the class of semi-slaves called "yanacuna". Their exact place in Inca society has not been clearly explained by the chroniclers.

Skillful artisans and craftsmen were delivered by their curacas to the court of the Inca in Cuzco, where they remained part of their lives.

Soldiers returning from distant lands had broadened their horizons through new experiences. If they had been rewarded for bravery, they acquired greater prestige in their native community.

In one word, it was a new social world, with an intensified horizontal and vertical social mobility.

(c) The economic reforms of the Incas have been frequently described by students of the Andean area. It will suffice to recall that the Incas divided the land of the conquered natives into three parts, the products of which were reserved for the Inca, the Cult of the Sun, and the community itself. It is not known whether these shares were equal in size. In bad years, the natives could exist on the supplies stored in the granaries of the Inca and of the Sun. In the years of satisfactory crops, however, about two-thirds of the products went to the state.

AGRI

Idleness was considered a major sin in the Inca Empire. According to Cieza de Leon,

Huayna Capac often said that to keep the people of those kingdoms under subjection, it was a good thing, when they had no other work to do, to make them remove a hill from one place to another. . . .[24]

José de Acosta tells us that

. . . they had searchers to examine if people employ themselves in works and punished the negligent. . . .[25]

According to Garcilaso de la Vega:

. . . he who neglected to irrigate his lands within the allotted time was severely punished. He received three or four blows across the shoulders with a stone; or was flogged over the arms and legs with ozier wands as an idle lazy fellow. . . .[26]

MINE

Men were drafted to work in the mines, to participate in royal hunts, to work on the construction of fortresses and other build-

---

[24] Pedro de Cieza de Leon, *op. cit.*, The Second Part, p. 209.
[25] Father José de Acosta. *The Natural and Moral History of the Indies*. Vol. 2, p. 421.
[26] Garcilaso de la Vega, *op. cit.*, Vol. 2, p. 14.

ings, to tend the llama-flocks of the Inca, and for many other tasks non-communal in scope.

The ayllus remained self-supporting just as they used to be, but over and above their needs, they had to produce for the state and for its numerous institutions.

(d) The introduction of the official Quechua language transformed the parochial native into a citizen of an Empire. However, the Quechua was probably not enforced by the Incas for the benefit of the natives. It was introduced to facilitate the administration of the Empire and the functioning of the armies.

(e) The annexation of a province was usually followed by the erection of a temple to the Sun and the forced introduction of the rites of the Inca religion. However, local ayllu divinities were not abolished and continued to hold the central place in the religious life of the natives. They were obviously more deeply rooted, as is evidenced by the fact that Spanish missionaries had to devote all their energy to the eradication of pre-Inca cults. The state religion of the Sun shared the destiny of the Empire and disappeared with it, almost without traces.

III. Organization of the Army and Conduct of Wars

In the foregoing chapters, we have discussed the methods and policies employed by the Incas for the consolidation of their power in their newly acquired territories. We have also made an attempt to analyze the changes that took place in the individual and communal life of the natives after their submission to Inca sovereignty. We shall next describe and analyze the functioning of the Inca military machine which made possible the successful military expansion of the Empire.

Soldiers

Every able-bodied man, living under the rule of the Incas, was subject to being drafted into the army, either for some particular campaign or for permanent service in the army. In this connection Garcilaso de la Vega indicated:

> . . . no one could be compelled to work at any craft but his own except the cultivation of the land and the duties of a soldier, for all men were liable to be called upon to perform their shares in these two employments. . . .[1]

The system of selection of soldiers in use in the Inca state is described in connection with the legendary Inca Huascar Titu Capac:

> . . . [he] commanded that the most robust young men of 30 years be sifted out in order that they might be instructed in warlike affairs by his captains, and [he ordered] the latter to make a report to him of this matter every month. And the drill was with bow and arrows, spears, spear-throwers, lances thirty palms long, and hardened bludgeons, all of these things being made with copper, and some of them with black palm-wood like a broadsword, so smooth and sharp that they cut as if they were of steel. . . .[2]

[1] Garcilaso de la Vega, *op. cit.*, Vol. 2, p. 46.
[2] Fernando Montesinos, *op. cit.*, p. 46.

Bartolomé de las Casas left a striking description of military training under the Incas:

In every settlement there were instructors in the art of fighting and of manipulating weapons. They had charge of all the boys from ten to eighteen, who at certain hours of the day, were ordered to fight among themselves in serious or sham-battles; those of the boys who proved stronger, braver, fiercer and more skillful in the art of fighting, were destined for a military career, in accordance with the orders of the king. . . . There was another method for testing the boys. . . . When they reached the age of eighteen they were aligned before a captain or a military instructor who would order a man with a club or some other weapon to "go over there and kill this man!"; the man so addressed would raise his club menacingly, as if he intended to strike. If the young man, who was on trial, showed any indication of fright on his face, he was discharged and sent away, to remain a peasant all his life. . . .[3]

Montesinos tells us that rivalry existed between soldiers of the two moieties of the settlement.

. . . as the whole kingdom was divided into these two sections wherever there were bands of soldiers, there was rivalry between the valiants of both parties.[4]

When a man was taken into the army, his family remained in the native ayllu and was taken care of by the village community.

The lands of soldiers who were employed in the wars were . . . tilled . . . like those of widows and orphans; and while the husbands were serving in the wars, their wives were looked upon as widows during their absence. Great care was taken of the children of those who were killed in the wars, until such time as they were married.[5]

The army maintained and enforced discipline, and desertion was a capital offense.

If any man returned from the war without permission, his captain or ensign accused him, and the decurion of his village [an official in charge of ten households] apprehended him. He was punished with death, for the treason of having deserted his companions and his captain in the

---

[3] Bartolomé de las Casas, *op. cit.* Chap. 5.
[4] Fernando Montesinos, *op. cit.*, p. 47.
[5] Garcilaso de la Vega, *op. cit.*, Vol. 2, p. 6.

war, as well as having abandoned the service of the Inca, or the general who represented him. . . .[6]

When the army was on the march,

. . . neither soldiers nor captains, nor even the sons of the Incas themselves were allowed to ill-use or oppress the people, or to take from them so much as a grain of maize; and if this command was infringed the punishment was death. Robbery was punished by whipping . . . and frequently the punishment of death was inflicted. . . .[7]

If there were any outbreaks of rebellion or mutiny, the principal ringleaders were brought to Cuzco, well guarded, where they were cast into a prison full of wild animals, such as serpents, vipers, tigers, bears and other evil creatures. . . .[8]

Soldiers were rewarded by the Inca, or by one of his representatives, for bravery. They received presents of clothes or other valuable objects and sometimes were given women from the Inca's House of the Chosen Women.

Officers

The chroniclers used Spanish military nomenclature in speaking of the commanders and officers of the Incaic armies. Naturally, such categories as "generals", "masters of the camp", "sergeants", and "ensigns", must be accepted as vague approximations to the officers' ranks that might have existed among the Incas. One basic distinction stands out, however, in the many descriptions, namely, the difference between the junior commanders, who were men of native origin and became officers by appointment, and the higher officers, who were members of the ruling Inca caste. Garcilaso de la Vega gives us an idea of this distinction in the following passage:

The captains of different ranks . . . succeeded to their offices by hereditary descent. They did not pay tribute but were considered exempt and were maintained from the stores in the royal depots.

But the officers below the rank of captain, who commanded from ten to fifty men were not free from tribute, not being of noble families. The generals and masters of the camp had the power to appoint the subordinate officers. . . .[9]

---

[6] Garcilaso de la Vega, *op. cit.*, Vol. 1, p. 153.
[7] Pedro de Cieza de Leon, *op. cit.*, The Second Part, p. 74.
[8] Pedro de Cieza de Leon, *op. cit.*, The Second Part, p. 74.
[9] Garcilaso de la Vega, *op. cit.*, Vol. 2, p. 39.

Whenever the curacas were given military ranks and functions by the Incas, they still remained under the direct control of commanders of noble origin. All really responsible tasks such as reconnoitering and espionage were entrusted to men of Inca blood only. Likewise, in battles, particularly arduous tasks, such as storming a well-defended mountain fortress, were assigned to detachments composed exclusively of the Incas. The Inca formed, thus, the real backbone of the Imperial Army.

Division of the Army into Units

As has been mentioned before, when the Spaniards came to Peru they found there a well-developed administrative system based on the decimal principle of grouping. Ten households formed the basic unit of this structure rising through a series of successive grades of 50, 100, 500, 1000, 5000 and 10,000 households or heads of families. The Empire as a whole ("Ttahuantin-suyu" meaning "land of the four sections") was divided into four quarters, headed by the highest ranking officials or "Viceroys", whose title in Quechua was "Apu-cuna". The Sapa Inca himself stood at the head of this pyramiding bureaucracy.

As indicated previously, the numerical nomenclature may not have been carried out literally, but it is certain that a system of graded hierarchical administration did exist for some length of time. It is important to point out that this administrative apparatus functioned not only for peacetime affairs but was also the backbone of the Inca military machine.

In an analysis of the Inca political system, it is extremely difficult to separate the military side from the non-military one. This may be due to the fact that the principal objective of Incaic policies, was the preservation and further expansion of their Empire. Just as every subject of the state was liable to be drafted into the army, so all the administrative units, together with their officials of every rank and grade, were expected to fulfill military functions whenever the need arose. Every element in the structure of the state served the purposes of war whenever needed. Thus, in the descriptions of the subdivision of the Inca army into units, it is not always clear whether the general administrative system or the army pattern is meant. The following account by Cieza de Leon illustrates this point:

The Kings established the following order in their wars, that the great concourse of people might not cause confusion. In the great square of Cuzco was the stone of war, in the shape of a sugar loaf, well enclosed and full of gold. The King came forth, with his councillors and favorites, to a place where the chiefs of provinces were assembled, to learn from them who were most valiant among their people, and best fitted to be their leaders and captains.

One Indian had charge of ten men, another received authority over fifty, another over a hundred, another over five hundred, another over a thousand, another over five thousand and another over ten thousand. All these had authority over men of their own tribe, and all obeyed the captain general of the king.

Thus if it was intended to send ten thousand men to any battle or campaign, it was only necessary to open the mouth and give the order; and the same with five thousand and any other number; and in the same way with smaller parties for exploring the ground or going the rounds, when fewer men were required.[10]

We cannot feel quite certain as to what was the real situation: Was the army organization patterned on the decimal system? Was there actual overlapping of administrative units and military subdivisions? Was there an approximate structural similarity between the military and the administrative hierarchies? These questions cannot be answered on the basis of available data.

That the armies were also subdivided along regional and tribal lines is suggested by a quotation from Cieza de Leon:

Each tribe was also distinguished by difference in the headdress. If they were *Yuncas* of the coast, they went muffled like gypsies. The *Collas* wore caps in the shape of a pump box made of wool. The *Canas* wore another kind of caps, larger and of greater width. The *Canaris* had crowns of thin lathes, like those used for a sieve. The *Huancas* had short ropes, which hung down as low as the chin, with the hair plaited. The *Canchis* had wide fillets red or black, passing over the forehead. These and all other tribes were known, one from the other, by their headdresses, and these were so clear and distinct that, when 15,000 men assembled, one tribe could easily be distinguished from another.[11]

Tribal consciousness must have been quite strong to judge by Cieza de Leon's account of how the Sapa Inca was eager to ingratiate himself with his warriors:

---

[10] Pedro de Cieza de Leon, *op. cit.*, The Second Part, p. 73.
[11] Pedro de Cieza de Leon, *op. cit.*, The Second Part, p. 72.

... to delight them, [the Inca] came forth each day in a new dress, such as that which was the special costume of the nation that he wished to honor on that day. Next day he put on another, always wearing that of the tribe which was invited to the entertainment and drinking bout. By this means he pleased them, and as much as it was possible, he endeared himself to them. . . .[12]

Pachacuti Yamqui tells us also that

... each nation and province [of the Inca state] had its war songs and musical instruments. . . .[13]

The Sapa Inca as Supreme Commander of the Army

In any discussion of military history, it is extremely important to establish in which organ of the state the power of war making was lodged. In the absolutist Inca state, it was the head of the state, the all-powerful Sapa Inca, who took the initiative in deciding upon war and peace. This refers obviously to offensive wars only, for in defensive wars the decision to make war was forced upon the state by the aggression of the enemy. Almost all known Inca wars, however, were campaigns of expansion, undertaken deliberately by the Incas themselves. The war against the Chanca rebels is one of the outstanding exceptions to this rule. Other defense actions were engaged in by frontier garrisons against the unsubdued hostile tribes living outside Inca territory.

The chronicles represent most Inca wars as individual undertakings by different Inca rulers. We must be aware, however, of the presence in Cuzco, in the Sapa Inca's surroundings, of important pressure groups reaping benefits from wars of expansion. Their role will be analyzed and discussed subsequently.

In numerous cases Sapa Inca headed his army as its commander-in-chief. At such times, he traveled in great luxury and with an elaborate retinue.

All being ready, the Inca set out from Cuzco in a litter enriched with gold and precious stones, which was surrounded by his guards with halberds, axes and other arms. Next to him marched the lords. . . . The Coya (his wife and the Queen of the Empire) and the other women

---

[12] Pedro de Cieza de Leon, *op. cit.*, The Second Part, p. 153.

[13] Santa Cruz Pachacuti Yamqui Salcamayhua, Juan de. *An Account of the Antiquities of Peru.* London, 1873, p. 116.

traveled in hammocks, and it is said that they carried a great quantity of jewels and of stores. In front, men were sent forward to clear the road, so that neither grass nor stone, large or small, might remain on it. . . .[14]

Inca Huayna Capac was said to have set out for Quito at the head of his army, taking with him two thousand concubines and countless servants.

The camps of the Sapa Inca were elaborate affairs, as can be judged from a description by Cieza de Leon:

When he [Inca Tupac Inca] reached the borders of the valley of Huarco [now known as Cañete], on the skirts of a mountain, he ordered a city to be founded, to which he gave the name of Cuzco, intending it to be his principal residence. The streets and hills and open squares received the same names as those of the real city. He said that until Huarco was conquered, and the people had become his subjects, he would remain in that place. . . . In the summers the Inca went to Cuzco, leaving a garrison in the new Cuzco that he had built, so that there might always be troops opposed to the enemy. . . . The valley having been subdued . . . he ordered the new Cuzco which he had built to be pulled down, and returned with his army to the city of Cuzco.[15]

The Sapa Inca is often represented as directing military operations, and at times even participating in actual fighting. It is possible that the controlled history of the Inca state ascribed more deeds of valor to the Sapa Incas than they really deserved. We know that most of them lived to a ripe old age, in spite of their participation in frequent wars.

The Inca heir was attached to the army in order to get experience in warfare, and it is probable that he participated in direct fighting sometimes, as was recorded by some chroniclers. The heir to the throne was often appointed commander-in-chief of an army, when his father for some reason had to stay in Cuzco. The brothers of Sapa Inca were also often appointed generals or supreme commanders.

As far as we can gather, the main function of the Sapa Inca, or of one of his sons and brothers, when he headed the army at war, was political and diplomatic in nature. In an army consisting of soldiers gathered from numerous tribes, who spoke different languages and

---

[14] Pedro de Cieza de Leon, *op. cit.*, The Second Part, p. 147.
[15] Pedro de Cieza de Leon, *op. cit.*, The Second Part, p. 192–193.

emanated from the four quarters of the Empire, the presence of the Sapa Inca was a unifying and a consolidating factor. During a campaign, the army had to conduct negotiations and to conclude agreements and alliances with the chiefs and the heads of the native tribes and states. The Sapa Inca, as well as his brother or son, had the necessary authority and prestige to fulfill this function.

One of the most interesting examples of an accord that was concluded during a military campaign, is contained in the chronicles of Garcilaso de la Vega. This example refers to the brother and son of Inca Pachacutec who negotiated with Cuismancu, lord of the Valley of Pachacamac.

. . . the Incas marched to the valley of Pachacamac and the chief Cuismancu advanced to defend his territory with a large force. The Inca general [Sapa Inca Pachacutec's brother Inca Capac Yupanqui] sent to him to say that it would be well not to fight until they had conversed more fully on the subject of their gods. . . . The Inca general also declared that hitherto the Kings Incas adored Pachacamac as the creator and sustainer of the universe, but that henceforth they would also look upon the Rimac, whom the Yuncas [the people of the valley of Pachacamac] worshipped, as a sacred oracle. And he proposed by way of brotherly exchange, that they should also take the Sun as a god. . . . The Yuncas agreed to worship the Sun like the Incas. . . . The King Cuismancu was to remain in the enjoyment of his lordship. . . . Peace was established on these conditions . . . proper garrisons and officers . . . placed in the new territory, the Inca Capac Yupanqui returned to Cuzco with the prince his nephew to report to the Inca his brother. . . .[16]

The conclusion of an agreement with Cuismancu, lord of Pachacamac, was followed by an Inca campaign against the Great Chimu, ruler of five thickly populated and fertile valleys. On this occasion, Cuismancu, lord of Pachacamac, sided with the Incas:

. . . [he] displayed great animosity against the powerful Chimu because, in times past, before the appearance of the Inca, he had waged a cruel war against them, making slaves of his prisoners and forcing them to be his vassals. . . . This war was very bloody among the Yuncas owing to their ancient enmity, and they served the Incas with more zeal than any other nation. . . .[17]

---

[16] Garcilaso de la Vega, op. cit., Vol. 2, p. 189.
[17] Garcilaso de la Vega, op. cit., Vol. 2, p. 196.

The above instances demonstrate the importance of diplomacy in the wars of the Incas, and explain the presence of the Inca, or his near kin, at the head of the army. While the army was the tool of Inca expansion, this tool had to be manipulated by expert diplomatists and politicians in order to be used effectively in the process of empire-building. No one could play this role with more authority than the Sapa Inca himself or some member of the ruling dynasty.

Economic Organization of the Army

The wars of the Incas were by no means improvised affairs. Previously, we described the construction of strategic roads, the widespread frontier fortresses and garrisons, the training of young men for service in the army, and other elements in the vast complex of activities, which made the Empire ever ready to repulse an aggression or to set out on a new campaign of expansion.

One of the essential prerequisites for an efficient army is a well-functioning commissariat. The Empire of the Incas solved this problem in the most efficacious way, as can be seen from the following account by Cieza de Leon:

. . . in each province there were a great number of storehouses for provisions and other necessities for a campaign, and for the equipment of soldiers; if there was a war these great resources were used where the camps were formed, without touching the supplies of allies, or drawing upon the stores of different villages. . . .

Then the storehouses were again filled from the obligatory tributes; and if by chance, there came a year of great sterility the storehouses were, in like manner, ordered to be opened, and the necessary provisions were given out to the suffering provinces. But as soon as a year of plenty came, the deficiencies so caused were made up.[18]

These storehouses, which were always well stocked, were situated at a day's marching distance from one another. When Pizarro and his companions landed in Peru, they found several of these in perfect condition, bursting with supplies.

Previously, we mentioned the fact that the land of village communities was divided by the Incas into three sections, the products of which were reserved for the Sapa Inca, the Cult of the Sun, and

---

[18] Pedro de Cieza de Leon, *op. cit.*, The Second Part, pp. 57–58.

the villagers themselves, respectively. Food supplies for the army storehouses were taken from the Sapa Inca's crops and also from the fields of the Sun.

The crops of the Sun and of the Sapa Inca in the region surrounding Cuzco, were earmarked for a special destination. Instead of being stored in the army granaries, along the roads, these were brought

. . . for the use of the court and that the Inca might have the means of feeding the captains and curacas who came to him.[19]

This commissariat set-up ended, of course, at the borders of the Empire. The Inca armies, bent on expansion and accustomed to fight on the territory of their neighbors, had to be followed across the borders by trains of supplies. The chronicles frequently speak of groups of porters following the armies and carrying loads. The Andean beasts of burden, the llamas, were much more useful in this respect.

Only strong male animals were selected for this service. Their carrying capacity was estimated at from two to eight "arrobas", a Spanish weight of twenty-five pounds, per beast, and from two to ten "leguas", a Spanish measure of nearly four English miles, a day. Since the llamas graze only during the day, their working capacity is limited, unless part of the march is accomplished at night. It is true, however, that they can get along without food for two or three days at a stretch. Flocks of llamas carrying burdens must be cared for by drivers at the approximate ratio of one man for fifteen animals.[20] Pizarro's lieutenant and historiographer, Don Francisco de Xeres, recorded in his memoirs, that when the Spaniards first encountered the army of the Inca Atahualpa at Cajamarca, this Inca's camp was so full of llamas that it was difficult to walk about. . . .[21]

As was stated before, the food of the storehouses was provided by the village communities along the roads. Other supplies were delivered to the state in the form of tributes by every province according to the raw materials available.

---

[19] Garcilaso de la Vega, *op. cit.*, Vol. 2, p. 24.

[20] For further details, see J. J. von Tschudi, *Das Lama*, *Zeitschrift fur Ethnologie*, 1885, pp. 93–109.

[21] Xeres, Francisco. *Reports on the Discovery of Peru*, London, 1872, p. 59.

. . . each province furnished its own produce, without seeking in any strange land for what it did not yield itself, for no province had to supply anything that did not belong to it. Thus they paid their tribute without having to leave their homes and it was the universal law throughout the empire that no Indian should be obliged to go beyond his own home to seek what he had to furnish as tribute. For the Inca said . . . that such demands would open the door to people wandering about from place to place and becoming vagabonds. . . .[22]

The cloth, in all parts of the sierra, was made of wool which the Inca supplied from his innumerable flocks, and those of the Sun.

On the plains of the sea coast, where the climate is warm and they do not dress in woolens, they made cotton cloths, the cotton being provided from the crops of the Inca and the Sun. . . .

They made three kinds of woolen cloth. . . . The fine cloth was made in the provinces, where the natives were most expert and handy in its manufacture, and the coarse kind was woven in the districts where the natives had less skill. . . .

The shoes were made in the provinces where the materials for making them were most abundant. In some they made bows and arrows, in others lances and darts, in others clubs and axes, in others slings and lashings, in others shields. . . .

Thus they had four things to supply to the Inca, namely provisions from his own lands, cloth made from the wool of the royal flocks, arms and shoes, according to the products of their respective districts. . . .[23]

Weapons

A methodical description of the weapons of the Incas requires a special study based on all available historical, archaeological and ethnographic evidence. It would not be pertinent to the problem at hand to offer more than a few data on this subject.

Bartolomé de las Casas gives us an idea of the order in which various arms were used in an encounter with the enemy.

. . . when they began to fight, at first they used slings with which they were extremely skillful and could shoot an infinite number of stones . . . as they got closer to each other they fought with lances; finally, they resorted to hand to hand fighting and used knobbed clubs and other weapons. . . .[24]

---

[22] Garcilaso de la Vega, *op. cit.*, Vol. 2, p. 19.
[23] Garcilaso de la Vega, *op. cit.*, Vol. 2, p. 18.
[24] Bartolomé de las Casas, *op. cit.*, p. 48.

They also used bows and arrows and "ayllos", a kind of bolas.

All these arms were known over the entire area of Inca expansion and there were few cases where they or their adversaries could be in a position of inferiority because of weapons. Nevertheless, some descriptions point to situations where two sides did fight with different arms, as for instance, in the case described by Sarmiento de Gamboa:

> The two armies approached each other in Ichupampa, encountered and mixed together, the Chancas thrusting with long lances, the Incas using slings, clubs, axes and arrows, each one defending himself and attacking his adversary. . . .[25]

The Incas carried little round shields of palm and cotton and also wore armor for protection against blows, darts, and arrows.

> [Huascar Titu Capac] invented the defensive arms, which were certain cloaks of fine cotton, wound about the body in many turns, and having above the breast and shoulders great plates; the Lords wore gold ones, the people of their blood and their captains wore silver ones, and others wore copper ones. . . .[26]

The Transportation of the Army

We have already discussed the intricate network of roads. These enabled the Incas to send their troops to any point within their Empire. When the necessities of the expansion led them across their borders, they overcame the difficulties of the terrain by improvised means, using their soldiers as workers. We can take the following illustration of their ingenuity from the chronicles of Garcilaso de la Vega.

> [After having occupied and pacified the province of Chumpivillca, Inca Mayta Capac] . . . marched across the uninhabited part of Cunti-suyu, a distance of sixteen leagues and encountered a formidable swamp three leagues broad, which checked the progress of the army. The Inca ordered a causeway to be made of large and small stones between which clods of earth were placed instead of mortar. The Inca himself worked at this causeway as well to give an example of industry as to assist in raising the large stones which were necessary for the work. Encouraged by his example, the people worked so hard that it was finished in a few days,

---

[25] Pedro de Sarmiento de Gamboa, *op. cit.*, p. 95.

[26] Fernando Montesinos, *op. cit.*, p. 46.

being six varas [variable unit of length, about 2,8 ft.] wide and two high. The Indians held and still hold this causeway in great veneration. . . . The duty of repairing this work is divided amongst different districts, each one undertaking a certain portion. . . .[27]

This same Inca Mayta Capac is described by Garcilaso de la Vega as an expert builder of military bridges:

. . . he ordered provisions and troops to be collected for new conquests . . . because he wished to march to the westward of Cuzco where is the region of Cunti-suyu, containing many large provinces. As it was necessary to cross the river Apurimac, he ordered a bridge to be made for the passage of the army. . . . In the time of the Incas these bridges were renewed every year by the people of the neighboring provinces, among whom the supply of material was divided according to their proximity to the work and their means. . . .[28]

The Inca bridges were of the suspension type. They were made of aloe-fibre ropes and their maintenance required constant vigilance on the part of the Inca officials. Hundreds of such bridges are still in use in Peru where they serve to connect roads that are separated by rivers, running in deep gorges.

The Incas inhabited an area that was rich in lakes and rivers. At the height of their expansion they ruled over an area with a long shore line. Nevertheless, we cannot say that they were particularly good navigators. The only craft that they used for transportation by water was the characteristic "balsa," a raft made of bundles of bulrushes which quickly became water-logged and had to be hauled ashore to be dried. The Incas constructed fleets of such balsas and ferried their armies across lakes and rivers. Inca Tupac is said to have visited, by means of the balsas the islands of Ninachumpi and Avachumpi, identified by some scholars today as part of the Galapagos Islands archipelago.

Garcilaso de la Vega describes how the soldiers of Inca Huayna Capac made a pontoon-bridge of balsas.

He advanced with his troops to a great river (Marañon), where many balsas were collected. . . . The Inca, perceiving that it would be unadvisable to send his army across the river by fours and sixes in these balsas,

---

[27] Garcilaso de la Vega, *op. cit.*, Vol. I, p. 230.
[28] Garcilaso de la Vega, *op. cit.*, Vol. I, p. 226.

ordered a bridge to be made by joining them together like a hurdle floating on the water. The Indians, both soldiers and servants, worked so diligently that the bridge was finished in a single day. The Inca crossed with his army formed in squadrons and marched rapidly to Cassa-marquilla. . . .[29]

Reconnoitering of the enemy's territory

Whenever the Incas were planning a campaign against an unfamiliar country, they sent on spies and investigators ahead. The size of their army and the quantity of supplies to be carried in the army train, were determined by the information obtained through these spies. An account by Garcilaso de la Vega well illustrates this side of the Inca military system.

The Inca Yupanqui resolved, after four years had elapsed. . . . to make another conquest. . . . This was the subjugation of a great province called Chirihuana, which is in the Antis to the east of Charcas. With this object, the land being hitherto unknown, he sent spies who examined the country and its inhabitants . . . and returned with a report that the land was execrable, being covered with dense forests, morasses and lakes very little of which was available for cultivation. . . .

[The Inca] ordered ten thousand warriors to be assembled, with whom he sent masters of the camp and *captains of his own family*. . . . These officers departed, and having ascertained a part of the disadvantages of the Chirihuana province, they sent a report to the Inca beseeching him to order further supplies to be sent to them that they might not fall short, because that land would yield none. . . . They were accordingly plentifully furnished with provisions. . . .[30]

This preliminary reconnaissance of the enemy country was apparently considered very important, since spies were selected only from among the captains of "the Inca's own family" and "persons of the blood royal."

Whenever the terrain was particularly difficult, the spies went in groups and worked in coordination with one another.

From Atacama the Inca sent spies into the desert to discover a road to Chile, and report upon its difficulties, in order that the necessary precautions might be taken. Only persons of the blood royal were employed

---

[29] Garcilaso de la Vega, *op. cit.*, Vol. 2, p. 437.

[30] Garcilaso de la Vega, *op. cit.*, Vol. 2, p. 274.

on duties of such importance by these kings, to whom some were given as guides. They stopped every two leagues to send back reports of what they had seen, an arrangement which was necessary in order that needful supplies might be sent. Yet the discoverers encountered great hardships and difficulties in the desert; and they set up marks so as to find the road on their return; and that those who should follow them might know whither they had gone. Thus they went backwards and forwards like ants, sending back reports of their discoveries, and bringing forward all necessary supplies. By these means they traversed the eighty leagues of desert between Atacama and Copayapu [Copiapo] which is a small but populous district, surrounded by wide uninhabited tracts; for beyond, as far as Cuquimpu [Coquimbo], there are other eight league of desert. After the discoverers had reached Copyapu, and collected all the information they could gather respecting the province, they returned, with all diligence, to make a personal report to the Inca. . . .[31]

The Strategy and the Tactics of the Incas

An adequate discussion of this subject should be undertaken by a professional military man familiar with the military techniques and ideas of Spain of the fifteenth and sixteenth centuries. Inca wars are known to us only from accounts of the Spanish chroniclers. Without a working knowledge of Spanish ideas and traditions concerning war, it is difficult to separate the Inca elements from the Occidental preconceptions expressed in the records. Only a few remarks of a non-technical nature can be offered in this study.

As far as we know, the arms and weapons used by the Incas were not substantially different from those of their enemies. Thus, in so far as military equipment was concerned, the Incas and their opponents were equally well outfitted. Under these circumstances, it was important to possess at least numerical superiority. Thanks to their efficient organization in the commissariat and in the transportation, the Incas were in a position to concentrate large armies at one point and to overwhelm their opponents with sheer numbers. Several accounts to this effect can be found in the chronicles. Sometimes the Incas merely brought their forces close to the enemy borders and abstained from fighting in the hope that the enemy would soon realize the futility of resistance.

Polo de Ondegardo considered that the Incas achieved only their

---

[31] Garcilaso de la Vega, *op. cit.*, Vol. 2, p. 278.

first victories by hard and hazardous fighting, and attributed their subsequent successes to their numerical superiority.

> There was no general opposition to their advances, for each province merely defended its land without aid from any other; so that the only difficulty encountered by the Incas was in the annexation of the districts around Cuzco. Afterwards all the conquered people joined them so that they always had a vastly superior force. . . .[32]

In addition to the numerical factor, Inca armies were said to be better disciplined than those of their neighbors. This opinion is further enhanced by what we know of the order and discipline in the administrative and economic life of the Inca state.

On the other hand, Inca warriors were men taken away from their native villages to fight for an alien cause, while their enemies were fighting for their own lands and homes. It is not unreasonable to assume that in their struggle against the Incas, the natives made up in ardor and stubbornness what they lacked in training and discipline.

One gets the impression from the chronicles that Inca war leaders were superior strategists. Since they were invariably the invaders, they had to conduct wars in unknown territories, fighting against native inhabitants familiar with the particularities of the terrain. This handicap did not prevent them from defeating the natives, in the majority of cases. Sarmiento de Gamboa left an account, however, of one of the rare instances where the Incas failed.

He describes the expedition undertaken by Tupac Inca against the natives of the "montaña", the thickly forested slopes of the eastern Andes.

> Tupac Inca . . . raised a powerful army which he divided into three parts . . . all these routes were near each other, and the three divisions formed a junction three leagues within the forest, at a place called Opatari whence they commenced operations against the settlements of the Antis. . . .
> The forests were very dense and full of evil places; so that they could not force their way through, nor did they know what direction to take in order to reach the settlements of the natives, which were well concealed in the thick vegetation. To find them the explorers climbed up the highest

---

[32] Polo de Ondegardo, *op. cit.*, p. 152–153.

trees, and pointed out the places where they could see smoke rising. So they worked away at road making through the undergrowth, until they lost that sign of inhabitants and found another. In this way the Inca made a road where it seemed impossible to make one.

Tupac Inca and his captains penetrated into this region of the Antis, which consists of most terrible and fearful forests with many rivers where they endured immense toil, and the people who came from Peru suffered from the change of climate, for Peru is cold and dry, while the forests of Anti-suyu are warm and humid. The soldiers of Tupac Inca became sick and many died. Tupac Inca himself, with a third of his men who came with him to conquer were lost in the forests and wandered for a long time without knowing whether to go in one direction or another. . . .[33]

This expedition culminated in a defeat. The armies of the Incas were outmanouevered by the environment. Their discipline and numerical superiority proved ineffective against the savage forest dwellers.

One of the frequently described tactical devices of the Incas consisted in their dividing their forces into several separate armies. The enemy was allowed to advance in full force and exhaust himself on one of the Incas' divisions. Thereupon, the Inca reserves would appear on the battlefield and administer a crushing blow.

Sarmiento de Gamboa describes how Inca Huayna Capac, at the siege of the fortress of the Cayambis, feigned flight and lured out the fortress garrison in pursuit of him. In the meantime, another detachment of the Incas, that had been held in reserve, occupied the fortress and defeated the Cayambis from the rear.[34]

Fortresses

Special consideration should be given to the role of fortresses in the expansion and defense of the Inca state. It has been an old Andean tradition to seek refuge in forts, "pucaras," situated on hill-tops. At the approach of the Inca armies, the natives with their families fled to these for cover. In these cases, the Incas waited patiently for the besieged natives to run out of food and either to attempt a sally or surrender.

The construction of very few fortresses of the Andean area can be definitely traced to the Incas. Most of these reveal earlier, pre-

---

[33] Pedro Sarmiento de Gamboa, op. cit., pp. 142–143.
[34] Pedro Sarmiento de Gamboa, op. cit., pp. 163–164.

Inca horizons; they apparently were only improved and enlarged by the Incas. After all, the Incas were late comers to this area, which was characterized by wars from at least the beginning of the Christian era. As mentioned previously, the very ancient (about 500 A.D.) Early Chimu pottery designs point to an old tradition of an elaborate and organized warfare.

The locations of the fortresses appear to have been adapted to geographical conditions. Thus, the fortresses of Sacsahuaman, on the heights overlooking Cuzco, of Machu Picchu, high above the Urubamba canyon, of Ollantaytambo, at the gates to the valley of Cuzco, and of Pisac, twelve miles from Cuzco constituted an ideal system of defense that effectively kept under control the Urubamba River corridor, leading from the eastern jungles to the fertile and densely inhabited valley of Cuzco.[35]

These, along with other ancient fortresses in the Andean area, must have been considerable obstacles to the process of Inca territorial expansion. But on the other hand, after they became parts of the Inca Empire, they must have served as powerful guarantees of Inca domination. They were permanently garrisoned by Inca soldiers and served as provincial centers of Inca control over the conquered populations. Those on the frontiers served another function, namely, that of protecting the Empire against the invasions of unsubdued neighbors. To study fortresses and other fortifications of the Inca Empire in connection with the history of its expansion, should prove an interesting problem for the archaeologists of the Andean area.[36]

Supernaturalism in Inca Wars

We have shown the Incas to be efficient and rational organizers and administrators in war and peace. Nevertheless, they too had their share of fears and anxieties in the conduct of wars. At Cuzco, as well as on the march with their army, the Sapa Inca was surrounded by priests, diviners, and magicians. Fernando Montesinos left a description of a technique that was used to foretell the outcome of a military undertaking.

---

[35] E. L. Hewett, Ancient Andean Life, pp. 250–262.

[36] For further discussion of Inca fortresses, see Max Uhle, Fortalezas Incáicas, Revista Chilena de Historia y Geografía, 1917.

They also used the wizards for foretelling the events of the future, and the secret method for learning certain events was to place in the fire a large flat earthenware vessel, which they call callana, containing a number of grains of maize of various colors, and each representing a person, in accordance with the name they gave it. The seer . . . urged it [the vessel and its contents] to give its answer by means of shaking. As soon as the grains [of maize] began to be shaken, some flew away from others, or drew nearer together. And if some grain failed to do what the seer commanded it was punished by him with a little rod, as if it were a person. . . .

If the King desired to learn of the outcome of some war, or battle or some other event, they placed the grains as usual, naming the captains [in charge of the forces] and saying certain words. The grains then had a great fight, some against others, until the conquered were driven out of the vessel, and then the wizard told the outcome as if he had seen it. . . .[37]

When at war, the Incas, as well as their enemies, considered themselves protected by tutelary supernatural spirits known in the Andean civilization as "huacas." The term "huaca" covered a wide range of objects that were supposed to be inhabited by an animated principle favorable to an ayllu. Portable huacas frequently accompanied the armies on the march and were carried by the priests.

Father José de Acosta describes a magical technique destined to neutralize the protective action of the enemy's huacas.

Those of Peru did sacrifice the birds of the Puna, for so they call the desert, when they should go to the wars, for to weaken the forces of their adversaries' Huacas . . . they took many kinds of small birds of the desert and gathered a great deal of thorny wood, which they called Yanlli, the which being kindled they gathered together these small birds . . . then did they cast them into the fire, about the which the officers of the sacrifice went with certain round stones carved, whereon were painted many snakes, lions, toads, and tigers, uttering this word Usachum (Usachuni— I accomplish), which signifies, let the victory be given unto us, with other words, whereby they said the forces of their enemies' Huacas were confounded.[38]

The Incas were also known to have practiced human sacrifices in order to propitiate the supernatural, but on a much smaller scale

---

[37] Fernando Montesinos, op. cit., pp. 88–89.
[38] José de Acosta, op. cit., Vol. 2, p. 342.

than the civilizations of Middle America. Most of the chroniclers were eager to exaggerate the inhumanity of the religion of the Incas; yet they failed to collect much evidence to this effect. There are surprisingly few references to human sacrifices in their writings. José de Acosta tells us a propos of this practice:

. . . the greatest part of these sacrifices were for the affairs that did import the Inca as in sickness for his health and when he went to the wars for victory . . .[39]

Sarmiento de Gamboa mentions human sacrifices resorted to by Inca Yupanqui during the war against the Collas:

. . . [he] made sacrifices "calpa" [means "force" or "army"] and buried some children alive, which is called "capa cocha," to induce their idols to favor them in that war. . . .[40]

The techniques of magic, diviniation, and propitiation illustrated by the above examples do not by any means exhaust the role of the supernatural in the military life of the Incas, whose religion was pervaded by militaristic ideas.

---

[39] José de Acosta, *op. cit.*, Vol 2, p. 344.

[40] Pedro Sarmiento de Gamboa, *op. cit.*, p. 122.

See also Polo de Ondegardo, *op. cit.*, pp. 165–166.

IV. The Determining Factors in the Military Expansion of the Inca State

This paper may be divided into three parts each of which corresponds to one aspect of the central problem.

In the first part,[1] the expansion of the Inca state was treated as a conflict between the various non-Inca societies and the Inca state. An attempt was made to analyze the methods to which the Incas resorted in their process of incorporating new peoples and new provinces into their Empire. On the other hand, attention was given to changes in the structure and life of the native societies under the impact of Inca domination.

The second part,[2] was devoted to the technical instrument employed in Inca territorial expansion, their military machine. An attempt was made to analyze structurally and functionally manifold activities connected with it, and to survey the various problems it had to solve.

The third part will take us to the political and geographical center, the source of Inca expansion, to Cuzco, the capital, and to the ruling Inca ayllus grouped about this city. An attempt will be made to analyze those economic, political, and ideological forces, associated with the interests and activities of the ruling caste, which were among the determinants of the Inca military expansion.

Economic Factors

Throughout the history of mankind warfare has so consistently been tied up with struggles for sources of wealth, that we hardly need justify our search for economic motives in the drive of the Inca state toward territorial expansion.

In discussing the material gains achieved through warfare, we should be quite specific in tracing the final destination of the

---

[1] Chapter II of this paper.
[2] Chapter III of this paper.

65

spoils and in establishing the identity of the distributors and beneficiaries of the newly acquired wealth and property.

In estimating the advantages derived from the territorial expansion of the Inca state we have to take into consideration the three basic strata of its population, namely, the Sapa Inca and his immediate family, the nobility (both of Inca and of native extraction), and the commoners.

a) THE SAPA INCA. The Sapa Inca was the absolute master of the Inca state and as such was identified with the state in all economic matters. All property of the state was ipso facto property of the Inca. Whenever additional wealth accrued to the state, the Sapa Inca obtained control over it. He was free to distribute any kind of property in the form of gifts and grants. That was the direct method of dispensing war spoils. There also existed, however, an indirect way of making men of his choice beneficiaries of the conquests. The administration of the new provinces created numerous posts with which went material advantages. All the principal appointments were made by the Inca personally and in this way his favorites shared in the good fortunes of the state.

Let us now survey the kinds of material gains made by the state and by the Inca as a result of the conquests.

In the first place, as we mentioned before, and as is well known from general descriptions, the land of the native ayllus was divided by the conquerors into three parts. The products of two out of three were surrendered by the natives to the state storehouses and granaries. These were used at the discretion of the state for the needs of the army, of the officials, and of the priests of the state-religion. When needed, they could be transported from one province to another and also to Cuzco. Thus, supplies of food were one of the basic and immediate gains achieved by the state and the Sapa Inca. Polo de Ondegardo describes the Inca's needs with regard to supplies of food:

> Another share of the produce was reserved for the Inca. This was stored in the granaries or sent to Cuzco, according to the necessities of the government. . . . The Inca supplied with food all his garrisons, his servants, his relations, and the chiefs who attended upon him, out of this share of the tribute, which was brought to Cuzco from all parts of the country.[3]

---

[3] Polo de Ondegardo, *op. cit.*, p. 156.

Another kind of property which came under the control of the Inca upon the occupation of a new province was the plantations of coca plants. Polo de Ondegardo's statement on this point is very clear:

> ... all the farms of coca belonged to the Inca ... in effect the Inca took the produce of all the coca farms throughout the Andes for his own use, except a few small patches granted to chiefs and officials. ... [4]

The third type of property which was confiscated by the Sapa Inca consisted of herds of llamas.

> The Inca did the same with all the males in the flocks, which were appropriated for the service of himself and of religion, being left, however, in the same district where they were bred, and merely counted. No female was included in the tribute. ... It was not all flocks, that were treated in this way; for a portion though a small one was left to the district and another to the chief, who afterwards granted some to his servants. ... There was a rule that females should never be killed, and thus the flocks multiplied exceedingly. ...
>
> A portion of the flocks of the Inca and of religion were also shorn, and cloth was made out of the wool and taken to Cuzco for the use of the Inca, and for the sacrifices. It was also used for clothing the attendants of the Inca or was stored in the magazine. ... [5]

Strict accounts were kept of the herds belonging to the Inca. Garcilaso de la Vega describes the system as follows:

> In order to preserve some account of the multitude of llamas belonging to the Incas, they were divided according to their colors. ... In this way they kept an account of the flocks with great ease, by means of their knots, the threads being dyed of the same colors as the flocks to which they referred. ... [6]

The fourth source of supplies consisted of the wild game. All private hunting was strictly forbidden and the communal hunting which was organized at definite seasons, was arranged to provide first for the needs of the Inca and then for the people.

After the tribute of the Inca and of religion had been paid, leave was given to supply the requirements of the people. Yet the game multi-

---

[4] Polo de Ondegardo, *op. cit.*, p. 158.
[5] Polo de Ondegardo, *op. cit.*, p. 158–160.
[6] Garcilaso de la Vega, *op. cit.*, Vol. 2, p. 29–30.

plied . . . far more rapidly than it was taken, as is shown by the registers they kept, although the quantity required for the service of the Inca and of religion was enormous. A regular account was kept of all the hunts, a thing which it would be difficult for me to believe if I had not seen it.[7]

The fifth type of property, limited by law to the Sapa Inca, consisted of gold and silver mines. These were worked under the supervision of the curacas. Since Indians who worked in the mines could not attend to the cultivation of their fields, the Sapa Inca compelled the neighboring provinces to provide labor for the sowing and reaping of the crops of the miners.

All gold and silver had to be delivered to Cuzco, the curacas being allowed to keep only small quantities for themselves. Upon delivery to Cuzco the gold remained there forever, unless, of course, otherwise ordered by the Inca.

. . . to add to the grandeur of their capital, a law was made that neither gold nor silver that once entered Cuzco should ever leave it again, on pain of death to be inflicted on the transgressor. Owing to this law, the quantity that entered being great, while none went out . . .[8]

The use of the precious metals was described by Garcilaso de la Vega thus:

In all the houses of virgins selected for the king, the utensils were of gold and silver, as in the houses of virgins of the Sun and in the famous temple, and also in the royal palaces. In short, it may be affirmed that all the wealth of gold and silver and jewels that was found in that empire, was used in no other way than in the adornment and service of the royal palaces. . . . The quantity used by the "curacas" was small being only for drinking cups and these were limited in size and number according to the privilege that the Inca may have granted to each. . . .[9]

At the death of the ruling Inca, all his treasures of gold and silver were given to his descendants, who preserved them along with his embalmed corpse. Thus, every new monarch was obliged to accumulate his own treasure of adornments, vases, jewelry, and other precious objects.

In addition to the sovereign rights that the Inca claimed on the

---

[7] Polo de Ondegardo, *op. cit.*, pp. 164–165.

[8] Pedro de Cieza de Leon, *op. cit.*, The Second Part, p. 40.

[9] Garcilaso de la Vega, *op. cit.*, Vol. 1, p. 302.

fields, flocks, game, the coca plantations, and the gold and silver mines, he expected, as a matter of course, valuable gifts from all those who came to Cuzco to pay him homage.

The curacas, lords of vassals, visited the Inca on the principal festivals of the year. . . . and on the occasion of triumphant celebration of victories, and when the heir to the throne was shorn and named, and on many other occasions during the year. . . . On all these occasions the curacas never kissed his hand without presenting him . . . with all the gold and silver and precious stones that their Indians could collect. . . . Besides these treasures, the curacas presented to their kings many kinds of precious woods for the palaces. . . . many wild animals, such as tigers, lions, bears, monkeys, cats, macaws, vultures . . . and condors. . . . They also presented large and small serpents. . . . They also brought great toads and lizards. The curacas from the sea-coast presented seals and alligators. . . . In short, there was nothing worthy of remark for its ferocity, size or beauty, which they did not present together with the gold and silver. . . .[10]

The above examples give an idea of the enormous wealth owned and controlled by the Inca rulers. The acquisition of every province represented for them new sources of wealth. In addition to the tangible property in the form of food, llamas, metals, etc., the Inca rulers, in conquering a new province, obtained control over additional labor. The tributes of the subjects were not limited to deliveries of goods, since they were also conscripted for work. Some men were removed from their homes permanently to join the class of the servants (yanacuna). They were sent to work on the private estates of the Inca and his relatives. Others were assigned to work at the court in the establishments connected with the Cult of the Sun.

The curacas were expected to send to Cuzco the best artisans and artists of their provinces:

. . . the men who excelled in any art, such as silversmiths, painters, singers and carpenters. . . . The common people did not require the aid of such artisans, because each Indian knew how to supply what he and his household needed; such as to make clothes and shoes, and to build a poor hut in which to live. . . .[11]

---

[10] Garcilaso de la Vega, op. cit., Vol. 2, p. 22.
[11] Garcilaso de la Vega, op. cit., Vol. 2, p. 22.

Cieza de Leon also describes the transfer of artisans from a newly occupied land:

The Inca's delegate remained in Chimu [upon its conquest by Tupac Inca Yupanqui] and the rest of the valley sent their tribute to Cajamarca. As the natives were expert in the working of metals, many were sent to Cuzco, and to the capitals of provinces where they worked gold and silver ornaments and vases, and any other things that were ordered. . . .[12]

The conscription of workers was not limited to individual artisans and artists. As we know, the Inca state was always engaged in ambitious public works such as building temples, palaces, fortresses, roads and irrigation canals. The conquest of new regions provided the Inca with fresh contingents of workers.

. . . provinces were required to send so many thousand laborers to Cuzco, to be employed on the public edifices of the city and of the kings, with supplies of their needful provisions. . . .[13]

And last, new provinces furnished more soldiers for further wars.

No attempt has been made in this study to give an exhaustive account of all the economic advantages gained by the Inca rulers through wars of expansion. The purpose of the above illustrations was to show only that, from the point of view of the Inca dynasty, military campaigns were unquestionably profitable undertakings. They provided Inca rulers with new property and sources of benefits, as well as with gifts, rewards and grants for distribution among their followers. Thus, it can be said with a reasonable degree of security that the Sapa Incas' lust for wealth and power was probably one of the determining factors in the military expansion of the Inca state.

b) THE COMMONERS OF THE EMPIRE. As far as the commoners were concerned, their direct participation in the spoils of war was limited to the rewards they received as soldiers for specific acts of bravery. Nevertheless, in the long run, the commoners as a group, also profited by the expansion of the Empire. The incorporation of new provinces into the system of interregional economic exchange favorably affected the less prosperous provinces which,

---

[12] Pedro de Cieza de Leon, *op. cit.*, The Second Part, p. 186.
[13] Pedro de Cieza de Leon, *op. cit.*, The Second Part, p. 54.

during years of poor crops, were enabled to depend on supplies of food from the more fertile parts of the Empire.

The great economic diversity of the provinces of the Empire allowed all of them to use a wider range of regional products. However, it remains to be demonstrated that the same results had not been achieved before the Inca domination. Archaeological evidence seems to point to the existence of trade contacts between different economic zones during early pre-Inca times.

Whatever profits the commoners did derive from wars of expansion, could scarcely be regarded as the actual goals of these wars. One could rightfully consider them as indirect consequences of the increasing prosperity of the Empire as a whole. It may also be added at this point, that the few material advantages gained by the commoners from the growth of Inca territory were out of proportion to their sacrifices. In the vast literature concerning the origins of wars much attention has been paid to the phenomenon of "population pressure". Although we know of a few instances where conquests opened new areas for settlement by Inca subjects, the total picture of Inca policies, and the limited number of recorded cases of economic colonization, do not encourage us to regard these as actual goals of Inca wars.

c) THE NOBILITY. The important role of the Inca ruling caste in the life of the Empire has been pointed out in this paper a number of times. There remains little to be added regarding the specific advantages they derived from wars of expansion.

When several Inca ayllus descended into the valley of Cuzco and imposed their domination over the aborigines, they were, in all probability, similar in many respects to those whom they conquered. They must have been democratic agricultural tribes looking for fertile lands, under the leadership of their sinchis, who were invested with greater or lesser authority.

After the initial conquests, the nucleus state of the valley of Cuzco grew and expanded; all the members of the master ayllus rose in rank and advanced economically. They gradually emancipated themselves from agricultural work and became dependent for their existence on the tributes of their subjects. The collecting of these tributes, the policing of the new provinces and the protection of the state against rebellions and aggressions, created numerous new offices. The members of the conquering Inca ayllus distributed among themselves these offices and the advantages connected with them. We have no data on the intermediary stages of this process, which the Spanish chroniclers found at the height of its development. When they landed in Peru, they found members of the ruling ayllus occupying all posts of responsibility and positions that conferred on their holders honors, influence, and wealth. The native provincial nobility was kept in the inferior ranks, subordinate to appointees of Inca blood. This was equally true of the three major branches of the state machine, the bureaucracy, the army, and the Cult of the Sun.

They had priests to offer the sacrifices. The priests of the House of the Sun at Cuzco were all Incas of the blood royal, and all those who performed other services in the temple were Incas by grant. They had a high priest, who was an uncle or brother of the king, or at least a legitimate member of the royal family. . . .

In the other provinces where there were temples of the Sun, which were numerous, the natives were the priests, being relations of the local chiefs. But the principal priest in each province was an Inca, who took care that the sacrifices and ceremonies should be in conformity with those of the metropolis.

For in all the chief offices, whether of peace or war, an Inca was placed as chief, the natives being in office under him.[14]

Speaking of the army, Garcilaso de la Vega makes a similar statement:

The same rule was observed in their wars, the native chiefs of the provinces whence troops were drawn never being deprived of the command of them. They were left in the enjoyment of their appointments, even if they were masters of the camp, while commanders of the blood royal were placed over them. They enjoyed serving under lieutenants of the Incas, whose members they said they were, being their ministers and soldiers; and they held such appointments being great favors.[15]

As we have already seen, there were two strata of nobility in the Inca Empire. The more influential group of nobles was made up of the descendants of the original conquerors and even the identity of the original invading ayllus was not lost among them. The bulk of their members lived in and around Cuzco.

---

[14] Garcilaso de la Vega, *op. cit.*, Vol. 1, p. 132.
[15] Garcilaso de la Vega, *op. cit.*, Vol. 1, p. 147.

The native nobility (the curacas) of the conquered provinces was encouraged to cooperate with the state and was compensated by being assimilated to the nobility of Inca blood.

Those who had worked most in the subjugation of the other Indians were allowed to imitate the Incas most closely in their badges and received more favors than the others.

Upon his accession to the throne, every Inca appointed a brother or some other close relative as head of his own ayllu, which was made up of his sons and of their male descendants in direct line. Since the Incas and their children were all polygamous, these royal ayllus grew very rapidly and developed into influential aristocratic lineages. Naturally, members of these ayllus were entitled to all choice rewards and appointments. A distinction seems to have been made between the children that the Sapa Inca had by his wives and those that he had by his concubines. Cieza de Leon describes this situation as follows:

The sons whom the lords had by these women, as soon as they were grown up, *received lands and fields*, which they called chacaras, and they were given clothes and other necessaries from the government stores for their use. But it was not thought fit that they should have lordships, because in the event of any troubles in the kingdom, it was not desired that they should be in a position to be looked upon as legitimate sons of the king. Thus *none of them was entrusted with the rule over a province*, although *in time of war many were captains* and were preferred to those who were of purer lineage. The legitimate lord who inherited them the kingdom favored them; but if they joined in any revolt they were cruelly punished.[16]

The favors accorded by the Inca to the nobles ranged from permission to travel in a litter and to dine on gold service to grants of estates with slave-servants.

Jose de Acosta reports in this regard:

. . . (those who) had done any good service in the war, or in the government of the commonweal, were honored and recommended with public charges, *with lands given them in proper*, with arms and titles of honor, and in marrying wives of the Incas' lineage. . . .[17]

---

[16] Pedro de Cieza de Leon, *op. cit.*, The Second Part, p. 27.
[17] José de Acosta, *op. cit.*, p. 423.

Garcilaso de la Vega also speaks of grants of land:

To the nobility such as the curacas, who were lords of vassals, were given lands varying in extent according to the number of their wives, children and servants; and the Incas of the blood royal received estates in the same way, wherever they desired to live. . . .[18]

This development of a landed nobility might have become an extremely significant phenomenon in the destiny of the state of the Incas. Unfortunately, information on this subject is fragmentary, and it has not yet been established whether a real class of land-owners was about to assume importance in the life of the Empire at the time when the Spaniards arrived.

Among the various forms of grants and rewards accorded to the nobles by the ruling Inca, clothing, arms, objects of gold can be mentioned. He also gave them Chosen Virgins of the Sun as brides. The most important rewards, however, consisted of appointments to lucrative posts and positions of influence.

It must be remembered that most of the nobles were polygamous and had the responsibility of large families.[19] They formed a rapidly growing class which was detached from all activities that were directly productive. They depended for their existence mainly on the state and the Sapa Inca, and their demands and claims might be regarded as a case of "population pressure" of a special kind.

As long as the Empire was expanding, there were always new fields of activity and new sinecures for Inca officials, army captains, and church dignitaries. If the process of territorial expansion had ceased for any considerable length of time, the nobles and their sons would have been disappointed in their expectations.

The chronicles contain several accounts of revolts and other difficulties among the nobles of Cuzco. Most of these difficulties seem to have been connected with dynastic rivalries and with each one of the various groups supporting their favorite legitimate heir, since the Inca could appoint any one of his sons as heir to the throne.

---

[18] Garcilaso de la Vega, op. cit., Vol. 2, p. 10.

[19] As indicated previously, Inca men married not only Inca women, but also native women who were reared in the Houses of the Chosen Women. (Inca women could marry only men of Inca blood.) This arrangement made possible an extensive polygamy among the Inca nobles and was a contributing factor to the numerical growth of the aristocratic caste.

As long as the process of territorial and economic expansion did not cease, all the careerists and trouble-makers could easily be satisfied and thereby neutralized. During lull period they were liable to grow restive. Exact data on the precise causes of trouble and dissatisfaction among the nobles are lacking, but from our general understanding of the situation, we may regard them as a turbulent and aggressive class, divided into competing hostile cliques. Successful military campaigns enriched the Sapa Inca and enabled him to keep his favorites and his kin satisfied. Acquisition of new provinces meant fresh sources of economic and bureaucratic advantages for the nobility of the Empire.

Centuries of development of social groups bent on satisfying their desires and appetites, could not fail to bring into existence among them of a corresponding system of values. Since these groups were in a position of power, their values assumed the characteristics of an official ideology. The last section of our study will be devoted to the discussion of the fragmentary evidence relating to this Inca ideology.

Ideological Factors

When we speak of the ideology of the Incas we have in mind the ruling dynasty and the nobility of Inca blood. The upper classes of the Inca Empire that were made up of those two groups formed a world of their own. Their upbringing, their economic position, and their social role were so different from those of the common people, that it almost looked as if the Inca Empire had two distinct cultures existing side by side.

However, the cultures of the upper classes retained in some form or other, all those elements which characterized the culture of the commoners. The Inca aristocrats were not aliens to the Andean populations. Their more sophisticated culture was a product of a long process in the elaboration of simple native elements. They shared with the common people the pattern of material existence (food, weaving techniques, pottery, etc.), weapons of warfare, totemic beliefs, and magical practices. But over and above this common stock of cultural characteristics, during the centuries of their privileged social position, the nobles evolved administrative techniques and political ideas which were their very own, and which remained alien to the common people.

According to Garcilaso de la Vega, Inca Rocca was directly opposed to all popular education:

He ordered that the children of the common people should not learn the sciences, which should be known only by the nobles, lest the lower classes should become proud and endanger the commonwealth. The common people were ordered to be taught the employments of their fathers, which was enough for them. . . .[20]

Father Blas Valera credits this same Inca Rocca with the founding of the first schools for the children of the nobility. His account, as restated by Garcilaso de la Vega, is as follows:

Inca Rocca was the first who established schools in the city of Cuzco, in which the amautas [scholars, teachers] imparted their learning to the Inca princes of the blood royal, and to the nobles of the empire. The schools were not established for teaching letters, for these people had none; but to instruct the pupils concerning the rights, precepts and ceremonies of their false religion, and the principles of their laws and customs, with their correct interpretation. It was intended that they should thus attain a knowledge of the art of governing and become both more *refined and more assiduous in the military art.* The pupils were also taught the methods of computing time, and of recording events, by means of knots, as well as to converse with elegance and grace. . . . They were then instructed in the arts of poetry, music, philosophy and astrology. . . .[21]

The educational disciplines described above made up only part of the training of Inca young men. The chroniclers left detailed descriptions of the initiation ceremonies ("Huaracu") which all Inca nobles had to go through at puberty. From the ordeals and tests of which these ceremonies consisted we can see that Inca youths were trained from early childhood to endure the hardships and dangers of war:

. . . [they] had to pass through a very rigorous novitiate. They were examined in all the labors and emergencies that are likely to arise in war, whether under prosperous or adverse circumstances. . . . The honor or shame that the novices acquired in the trial was shared by their relations. . . .

---

[20] Garcilaso de la Vega, *op. cit.*, Vol. 1, p. 336.
[21] Garcilaso de la Vega, *op. cit.*, Vol. 1, pp. 336–337.

For six days the novices had to endure a very rigorous fast, during which time they were given nothing but a few grains of raw maize and a jar of plain water. . . . He who showed himself weakened and distressed by the fast, or who asked for more food, was reproved or expelled from the novitiate. . . .

After the fast . . . the novices were examined in the agility of their persons. As a test they were made to run from the hill called Huanacauri to the fortress of the city, a distance of nearly a league and a half. . . . The parents and relatives of the runners put before them the honor on the one hand and the shame on the other, representing to them that it would be less disgraceful to expire than to falter in the race. . . .[22]

The climax of these ceremonies was reached in a sham-battle between two groups of novices:

One was ordered to remain in the fortress and the other to go outside and to fight one against the other, one striving to take the fortress and the other to defend it. After the contest had lasted the whole day, they changed rounds on the following day, those who had been defenders taking the place of assailants, so that they might display their skill under various circumstances, as well in defending as in attacking strong places; In these fights . . . there were severe wounds given sometimes even causing death because the desire for victory excited them even to the point of killing each other. . . .[23]

These citations speak for themselves. Tests of military skill cannot be regarded as isolated episodes in the life of the young nobles. From their early years, their emotions, and their imagination must have been oriented toward these crucial "rites de passage," which opened to them the door of manhood and a dignified position in their caste.

The chroniclers emphasize the role of the families in encouraging the young contestants and identifying themselves with their successes or humiliations. This is an indication of the fact that honor and military courage were values recognized by the entire ruling caste.

The descriptions of the Inca celebrations of victories point in the same direction. Garcilaso de la Vega left an account which is particularly interesting in that it shows that victory was experienced as a group achievement:

---

[22] Garcilaso de la Vega, op. cit., Vol. 2, pp. 168–169.

[23] Garcilaso de la Vega, op. cit., Vol. 2, pp. 169–170.

All the people of the city marched in batallions according to the provinces of which they were natives, with their curacas leading them, with instruments such as drums, trumpets and shells, according to the usage in their own provinces; and new songs were composed with appropriate words, in praise of the excellent deeds of the captain general Capac Yupanqui, and of the prince his nephew, Inca Yupanqui. . . . Behind the captives and citizens came the soldiers with their weapons in their hands, marching according to their provinces, and also singing songs. . . . After the soldiers came the Incas of the blood royal, with weapons in their hands, as well as those who came out of the city as those who had been in the war, all marching together without distinction; *for any deed performed by a few or many Incas was looked upon as common to all and as if the whole family had been engaged in it.*[24]

We mentioned previously the "amautas" who were scholars and teachers in the Inca schools. They were also authors of the dramas which were performed at court. All actors were either noblemen of Inca blood or curacas. The subject matter of the dramas related to military deeds, triumphs and victories, as well as to the glories of the former ruling Incas or of other heroes in Inca history.

One of these dramas, "Ollantay," was preserved in the original Quechua language and became an object of heated debates between those who accepted and those who rejected its authenticity. It is curious to see that internal evidence proved of little avail in this learned discussion, for the pride of caste and the military spirit were almost equally characteristic of Spain of that period as of the Inca nobility. Consequently, it was difficult to identify the nationality of the author or plagiarizer. . . . It seems reasonable to accept the fact that while the drama, in its entirety, is a result of obvious Spanish retouching and rewriting, its songs and monologues are of Inca origin. And these songs and monologues are a striking expression of a militaristic caste ideology.[25]

Historical songs praising the military prowess of the Incas were composed by the officials in charge of the records of the Empire ("quipu-camayoc"), the official historians of the Incas.

---

[24] Garcilaso de la Vega, *op. cit.*, Vol. 2, pp. 144–145.

[25] For further discussion of the drama Ollantay see Cl. Markham, "Note on the Ancient Ynca Drama" in P. de Cieza de Leon's *Second Chronicle of Peru*, Hakluyt Society, London, 1883.

These knew how to narrate the events in regular order, like ballad singers and romance writers. . . . They were instructed what to say of the deceased lord [Inca] and if they treated of wars, they sang in proper order, of the many battles he had fought in different parts of the Empire. . . . These songs were not to be recited always and in all places; but only on occasions where there was a great and solemn assembly of people from all parts of the kingdom, or when the principal lords met together before the king on special occasions. . . . If any of the Inca's predecessors had been negligent, cowardly or vicious, or *preferred pleasure to the labor of extending the bounds* of the empire, it was ordered that such a king should receive little or no mention.[26]

In this chapter we have discussed (a) the Inca ideas concerning education, (b) their rites of initiation, with emphasis on fitness for war, (c) the group pride that they expressed in celebrating their victories, (d) the glorification of military valor in their songs and dramatic performances, and, finally, (e) the place of territorial expansion achieved by an individual ruler in their appraisal of this ruler's accomplishments.

These phenomena represent the little we know of Inca ideas, attitudes and emotions relating to warfare. Wars in general can be forms of group action caused by some definite and direct needs, and in such cases they may be free from any militaristic tinge. However, frequent participation in wars brings into existence a system of militaristic values and emotions; these become factors by themselves, sometimes independent of real economic or political needs and interests. It is probable that Inca wars cannot be explained entirely in terms of direct economic needs of the Inca dynasty and nobility. Several centuries of military history must have brought about an impetus of its own, in which ideas and emotions connected with war and bred by war, became actual determinants of further military adventures.

---

[26] Pedro de Cieza de Leon, *op. cit.*, The Second Part, pp. 28-29.

Appendix
The Dynastic History of the Incas

The history of the Inca Empire has been narrated by a number of able and competent authors, including Prescott, Markham, Joyce, Means and Cunow. In this essay I have avoided all reconstruction of historical sequences and have used historical data only in so far as they were related to my central problem. My interest has been confined to the social processes and institutions of the Andean area revealed or suggested by the chronicles, and no effort has been made to show the precise allocation of specific occurrences to definite Inca reigns. For the sake of chronological orientation, however, this appendix has been added where a brief dynastic history of the Incas is outlined in a sketchy form.

All histories of the Inca dynasty begin with the myth of the Four Brothers and their Wives. There are a number of minor discrepancies among various chroniclers as to their personal names. The names of the brothers are preceded by the term 'Ayar', which according to Cunow means old relative or ancestor. The names of the four women are preceded by the term 'Mama', which has been translated by Cunow as denoting the speaker's mother, and by extension, a woman ancestor. These four mythical couples emerged from a 'House of the Dawn,' 'Paccari-Tampu', or, according to other versions, from a 'House of the Windows', 'Tampu-Tocco'. Only one of the four brothers, Ayar Manco Capac, who was married to his sister Mama Occlo, reached the City of Cuzco, where he finally settled down and became the founder of that glorious dynasty. Manco Capac's power was based on the possession of a fetish-bird called Inti (Sun). Although surrounded by obvious legends, Manco Capac may have been an actual historical figure, for there exist a number of rather realistic accounts of his struggles with the native ayllus of the valley of Cuzco.

The actual dynastic history of the Incas extended between the reign of this semi-legendary Inca and the landing of Pizarro and his band of 190 warriors at Tumbez in 1532. There is surprisingly little disagreement on the number and the order of succession of the Inca rulers between these two points. The majority of modern scholars accept the dynastic list of corresponding exactly to the one contained in the papers of the Viceroy Don Francisco de Toledo as well as in the chronicles of Sarmiento de Gamboa and in some other sources. According to this list, ten Sapa-Incas reigned between the time of the legendary Manco Capac and the arrival of the Spanish. They were as follows:

    I. Sinchi Roca
   II. Lloque Yupanqui
  III. Mayta Capac
   IV. Capac Yupanqui
    V. Inca Roca (Rocca)
   VI. Yahuar Huaccac
  VII. Viracocha Inca
 VIII. Pachacutec Inca Yupanqui
   IX. Tupac Inca Yupanqui
    X. Huayna Capac

Garcilaso de la Vega, Betanzos and Velasco split the eighth Sapa Inca's personality into two different men, Pachacutec and Inca Yupanqui; this variant, however, finds little favor with the scholars.

Another modification was offered by Cieza de Leon and Herrera who mentioned a short-lived reign of Inca Urco, following the reign of the seventh Inca Viracocha.

When Huayna Capac, the tenth Inca, died, his two sons (by different wives) Huascar and Atahualpa, ruled over two halves of the Empire and later on engaged in a fratricidal conflict, which was not ended until after the Conquistadores had arrived.

The remarkable unanimity on the subject of dynastic successions can be contrasted to the important disagreements on the distribution of specific historical events (mostly wars and conquests) in the reigns of the ten or eleven Incas. The so-called Toledan school, represented mainly by Sarmiento de Gamboa, and upheld today by Jijón y Caamaño, maintains that the tremendous military expansion of the Empire was the accomplishment of the eighth Sapa Inca Pachacutec Inca Yupanqui. The fact is, that this Inca's name is associated with a rich heroic folklore, and it is not completely unwarranted to regard him as an Alexander or a Napoleon of the Andes. Jijón y Caamaño advances several arguments in favor of the Toledan school, which believed in a relatively short duration of the Inca Empire of large dimensions.

(*a*) He is impressed by the uniformity of Inca pottery. In his own words, "it is impossible to tell an arribal (pottery vessel) of Cuzco from one of Quito or Northwest Argentina. This uniformity of style should be explained, he thinks, by a rapid spread of the Inca sovereignty over a vast territory. The same uniformity has been found by him in other arts, namely, masonry, weaving, etc.

(*b*) The survival of native Indian dialects in regions comparatively close to Cuzco, also demonstrates, in his opinion, a recent occupation of these areas by the Incas.

(*c*) The survival of the pre-Incaic religious cults and beliefs is another argument in favor of the short-lived expansion.

The so-called Garcilasan school is represented today by Philip Means whose criticisms of the above views have been summarized by Jijón y Caamaño[1] and run as follows:

(*a*) He finds the time between the beginning of Pachacutec Inca Yupanqui's reign and the Spanish conquest too short for the construction of the immense number of palaces, roads, aqueducts, and other monumental works of Inca style.

(*b*) He thinks that the victory over the Chancas (under Inca Viracocha, Pachacutec's predecessor) must have been accomplished by a state which was already very powerful.

(*c*) He questions the chronology of Sarmiento de Gamboa, according to whom Pachacutec lived 125 years and reigned 103 years.

(*d*) He points out that Sarmiento de Gamboa was influenced by the desire of the Viceroy Don Francisco de Toledo to prove that the Incas were tyrants and usurpers of power *of recent origin*.

(*e*) Finally, Means reminds us that Garcilaso de la Vega's chronology was based on the most reliable chronicles, which have since then been lost, by Padre Blas Valera.

---

[1] J. Jijón y Caamaño. *Los Orígenes del Cuzco*. Quito, 1934.

BIBLIOGRAPHY

ACOSTA, FATHER JOSÉ DE. The natural and moral history of the Indies. Edited by Clements R. Markham. 2 Volumes. Hakluyt Society. London. 1880.

ALVARADO, JULIO. La Société Quechua d'aujourdhui en Bolivie. Revue Anthropologique. No. 44, pp. 97-114. 1934.

AVILA, FATHER FRANCISCO DE. A narrative of the errors, false gods, and other superstitions and diabolical rites in which the Indians of Huarochiri lived in ancient times. Translated and edited by Clements R. Markham in Rites and Laws of the Incas. Hakluyt Society. London. 1873.

BANDELIER, ADOLF F. The Islands of Titicaca and Coati. New York. 1910.

BASADRE, JORGE. Historia del derecho Peruano. Volumen 1. Lima. 1937.

BASTIAN, ADOLF. Die Kulturländer des alten Amerika. 3 Volumes. Berlin. 1878-1889.

BAUDIN, LOUIS. L'empire socialiste des Incas. Travaux et Mémoires de l'Institut d'Ethnologie. Paris. 1928.

BETÁNZOS, JUAN DE. Suma y narración de los Incas. Edited by Don Marcos Jiménez de la Espada. Biblioteca Hispano-Ultramarina. Madrid. 1880.

BEUCHAT, HENRI. Manuel de l'archéologie américaine. Paris. 1912.

BINGHAM, HIRAM. The Inca Peoples and their culture. XIX International Congress Of Americanists. Pp. 253-260. Washington. 1917.

Inca Land. Boston. 1922.

Machu Picchu, a citadel of the Incas. New Haven. 1929.

BOWMAN, ISAIAH. The Andes of Southern Peru. New York. 1916.

Desert trails of Atacama. New York. 1924.

BUCHWALD, OTTO VON. Das Reich der Chimu. Globus. Pp. 149-151. 1909.

CARRIÓN CACHOT, R. La mujer y el niño en el antigüo Perú. Inca. Vol. 1. Lima. 1923.

CASAS, BARTOLOMÉ DE LAS. De las antigüas gentes del Perú. Madrid. 1892.

CHAMBERLAIN. Linguistic Stocks of South American Indians. American Anthropologist. 1913.

CIEZA DE LEON, PEDRO DE. The travels of Pedro Cieza de Leon. A. D. 1532-1550 contained in the First Part of his Chronicle of Peru. Translated and edited by Clements R. Markham. Hakluyt Society. London. 1864.

The Second Part of the Chronicle of Peru. Translated and edited by Clements R. Markham. Hakluyt Society. London. 1883.

COBO, FATHER BERNABÉ. Historia Del Nuevo Mundo., Edited by Don Marcos Jiménez de la Espada. 4 Vols. Sevilla. 1890-1893.

CÚNEO VIDAL, R. Del concepto del Ayllu. Boletín de la Sociedad Geográfica de Lima. Pp. 4-9. 1914.

Folk-Lore Andino. Inca. Vol. 1. Pp. 421-431. 1923.

CUNOW, HEINRICH. Die soziale Verfassung des Inkareiches. Stuttgart. 1896.

Geschichte und Kultur des Inkareiches. Amsterdam. 1937.

DIXON, ROLAND B. Contacts with America across the Southern Pacific. In The American Aborigines, Edited by Diamond Jenness. Toronto. 1933.

FARABEE, WILLIAM CURTIS. Indian tribes of Eastern Peru. Peabody Museum Papers. 1922.

FERRIS, H. B. The Indians of Cuzco and the Apurimac. Memoirs of the American Anthropological Association. Lancaster. 1916.

FRIDERICI, GEORG. Über die Behandlung der Kriegsgefangenen durch die Indianer Amerikas. Festschrift Eduard Seler. 1922.

GARCILASO DE LA VEGA. The First Part of the Royal Commentaries of the Yncas. Translated and edited by Clements R. Markham. Hakluyt Society. London. 1869–1871.

HAECKEL, JOSEF. Zweiklassensystem, Männerhaus und Totemismus in Südamerika. Zeitschrift für Ethnologie. Pp. 426–454. 1938.

HANSTEIN, OTFRID VON. The world of the Incas. Translated by Anna Barwell. London. 1925.

HARCOURT, RAOUL ET MARIE D'. La musique des Incas et ses survivances. 2 Vols. Paris. 1925.

HEWETT, EDGAR L. Ancient Andean Life. New York. 1939.

HOLSTEIN, OTTO. Chan-Chan, capital of the Great Chimu. Geographical Review, pp. 36–61. 1937.

HONIGSHEIM, PAUL. La cultura de América pre-colombina. Boletín Bibliográfico. Pp. 26–33. Lima. 1938.

Informaciones acerca del Señorio y Gobierno de los Incas hechas por mandado de Don Francisco de Toledo, Virey del Perú. Vol. 16 de la Colección de Libros Españoles Raros y Curiosos. Madrid. 1882.

JIJÓN Y CAAMAÑO, JACINTO. La religión del impero de los Incas. Vol. 1. Quito. 1919.
Los orígenes del Cuzco. Edición especial tomada de los "Anales de la Universidad Central" T. 52. No. 287. Quito. 1934.

JOYCE, THOMAS ATHOL. South American Archeology. London. 1912.

KARSTEN, RAFAEL. The civilization of the South American Indians. London. 1926.

KRICKEBERG, WALTER. Amerika, in Georg Buschan's Illustrierte Völkerkunde. Vol. 1. Pp. 52–427. Stuttgart, 1922.
Mexikanisch-peruanische Parallelen. Festschrift P. W. Schmidt. Wien. 1928.

KROEBER, A. L. Culture stratifications in Peru. American Anthropologist. Pp. 331–351. 1926.
Coast and highland in prehistoric Peru. American Anthropologist. Pp. 625–653. 1927.

KROEBER, A. L. AND STRONG, W. D. The Uhle collections from Chincha. The University of California Publications in Amer. Archeology and Ethnology. 1924.
The Uhle pottery collections from Inca. The University of California Publications in American Archeology and Ethnology. 1924.

LAFONE QUEVEDO, SAMUEL A. The great Chanca confederacy. International Congress of Americanists. Pp. 115–125. London. 1912.

LANGLOIS, LOUIS. "Parmonga." Rev. Mus. Nac. Lima. 1938.

LARCO HERRERA, RAFAEL. La civilità Yunga. International Congress of Americanists. Pp. 565–581. Rome. 1928.

LATCHAM, R. E. La existencia de la propiedad en el antigüo imperio de los Incas. Santiago 1923.
El dominio de la tierra y el sistema tributario en el antigüo imperio de los Incas. Revista Chilena de Historia y Geografía. Pp. 201–257, 1927.
The totemism of the ancient Andean peoples. Journal of the Royal Anthropological Institute. Pp. 55–87. 1927.
Los Incas, sus orígenes y sus ayllus. Revista de la Universidad de Chile. Vol. V. Pp. 1017–1054. 1927. Vol. VI. Pp. 159–233. 1928.

LOTHROP, K. Pottery of Costa Rica and Nicaragua. 2 Vols. Museum of the American Indian. New York. 1926.
Inca treasure as depicted by Spanish historians. Publications of the Frederick Webb Hodge Anniversary Publication Fund. Vol. 2. Los Angeles, 1938.

MACBRIDE, GEORGE McCUTCHEON. The agrarian Indian communities of Highland Bolivia. American Geographical Society. New York. 1921.

MARKHAM, CLEMENTS ROBERT. The Incas of Peru. London. 1910.
Vocabularies of the general language of the Incas of Peru or Runa Simi, called Quichua by the Spanish grammarians. London. 1908.
MEAD, CHARLES W. Old civilizations of Inca land. American Museum of Natural History. Handbook Series No. 11. New York, 1932.
MEANS, PHILIP AINSWORTH. Culture sequence in the Andean area. International Congress of Americanists. Pp. 236–252. Washington. 1917.
A study of ancient Andean social institutions. Transactions of the Connecticut Academy of Arts and Sciences. Pp. 407–469. 1925.
Biblioteca Andina. Transactions of the Connecticut Academy of Arts and Sciences. Pp. 271–525. 1928.
Ancient civilizations of the Andes. New York. 1931.
Fall of the Inca empire. New York. 1932.
MEILLET ET COHEN. Les langues du monde. Paris. 1925.
MIDDENDORF, E. W. Peru. 3 Vols. Berlin. 1893–1895.
MINNAERT, PAUL. Les institutions et le droit de l'empire des Incas. Bruxelles. 1928.
MOLINA OF CUZCO, FATHER CRISTOBAL DE. The fables and rites of the Yncas. Translated and edited by Clements R. Markham, in Rites and Laws of the Yncas. Hakluyt Society. London. 1873.
MONTELL, GÖSTA. Dress and ornaments in ancient Peru. Gothenburg. 1929.
MONTESINOS, FATHER FERNANDO. Memorias antiguas historiales del Perú. Translated and edited by P. A. Means. Hakluyt Society. London. 1920.
MURDOCK, GEORGE PETER. The organization of the Inca society. Scientific Monthly. Pp. 231–239. 1934.
The Incas of Peru. Chapter XIV in "Our Primitive Contemporaries." New York. 1934.
NORDENSKIÖLD, ERLAND. The copper and bronze ages in South America. Goeteborg. 1921.
The ethnography of South America. Goeteborg. 1924.
Origin of the Indian civilization in South America. Goeteborg. 1931.
Forschungen und Abenteuer in Südamerika. Stuttgart. 1924.
PIZARRO, PEDRO. Relation of the discovery and conquest of the kingdoms of Peru. Translated and edited by P. A. Means. New York. 1921.
POLO DE ONDEGARDO. Of the lineage of the Yncas and how they extended their conquests. Translated and edited by Clements R. Markham, in Rites and Laws of the Yncas. Hakluyt Society. London. 1873.
POZO, HILDEBRANDO CASTRO. Del Ayllú al cooperativismo socialista. Lima. 1936.
PRESCOTT, WILLIAM HICKLING. History of the Conquest of Peru. 2 Vols. New York. 1847.
REGAL, ALBERTO. Los Caminos del Inca en el Antigüo Peru. Lima. 1936.
RESTREPO, V. Los Chibchas antes de la conquista española. Bogotá. 1895.
SAAVEDRA, BAUTISTA. El Ayllu. La Paz. 1913.
SANTA CRUZ, ANTONIO. Land-tenure in pre-Inca Peru. New Mexico Anthropologist. Pp. 2–9. 1940.
SANTA CRUZ PACHACUTI YAMQUI SALCAMAYHUA, JUAN DE. An account of the antiquities of Peru. Translated and edited by Clements R. Markham, in Rites and Laws of the Yncas. Hakluyt Society. London. 1873.
SARMIENTO DE GAMBOA, PEDRO. History of the Incas. Translated and edited by Clements R. Markham. Hakluyt Society. London. 1907.
SCHMIDT, P. WILHELM. Kulturkreise und Kulturschichten in Südamerika. Zeitschrift für Ethnologie. Berlin. 1913.
SQUIER, E. GEORGE. Peru, incidents of travel and exploration in the land of the Incas. New York. 1877.

TELLO, JULIO. Andean Civilization. International Congress of Americanists. New York. 1928.
Antigüo Peru. Lima. 1929.

THOMPSON, J. ERIC. Archeology of South America. Field Museum of Natural History. Chicago.
1936.

TRIMBORN, HERMANN. Der Kollektivismus der Inkas in Peru. Anthropos. Pp. 978-1001. 1923-
1924.
Straftat und Sühne in Alt-Peru. Zeitschrift für Ethnologie. Pp. 194-240. 1925.
Familien und Erbrecht in prekolumbischen Peru. Zeitschrift für vergleichende Rechtswis-
senschaft. Pp. 352-392. 1926.
Die Gliederung der Stände im Inka-Reich. Journal de la Société des Américanistes de
Paris. Pp. 303-344. 1927.
Die Organisation der öffentlichen Gewalt im Inka-Reich. Festschrift P. W. Schmidt.
Pp. 740-759. Wien. 1928.
Kulturhistorische Analyse der altperuanischen Soziologie. International Congress of
Americanists. Pp. 415-424. Rome. 1928.
Die kulturhistorische Stellung der Lamazucht in der Wirtschaft der peruanischen Ernte-
völker. Anthropos. Pp. 656-664. 1928.
Unsere älteste ethnographische Quelle über das Inkareich. Zeitschrift für Ethnologie.
Pp. 402-416. 1934.
Quellen zur Kulturgeschichte des präkolumbischen Amerika. Stuttgart. 1936.

TSCHUDI, J. J. VON. Das Lama. Zeitschrift für Ethnologie. Pp. 93-109. 1885.

UHLE, MAX. Pachacamac. Philadelphia. 1903.
El aillú peruano. Boletín de la Sociedad Geográfica de Lima. Pp. 81-94. 1911.
Los orígenes de los Incas. International Congress of Americanists. Pp. 302-353. Buenos
Aires. 1912.
Fortalezas Incáicas. Revista Chilena de Historia y Geografía. 1917.

URTEAGA, HORACIO H. El ejército incáico, su organización, sus armas. Boletín de la Sociedad
Geográfica de Lima. Pp. 283-332. 1920.
Las antigüas civilizaciones y razas del Perú. International Congress of Americanists.
Vol. 2. Pp. 423-450. Rio de Janeiro. 1928.
El imperio incáico. Lima. 1931.

VALCÁRCEL, LUIS E. La religión de los antigüos Peruanos. Lima. 1939.

VERNEAU R., AND RIVET, P. Ethnographie ancienne de l'Equateur. Paris. 1912.

VIZCARRA, JULIO A. Las ideas religiosas en el antigüo Perú. Cuzco. Revista Universitaria. 1938.

WISSLER, CLARK. The American Indian. New York. 1931.

XERES, FRANCISCO DE. Narrative of the conquest of Peru. Translated and edited by Clements
R. Markham, in the Reports on the Discovery of Peru. Hakluyt Society. London.
1872.